Setting up Classroom Spaces That Support Students With Autism Spectrum Disorders

Setting up Classroom Spaces That Support Students With Autism Spectrum Disorders

Susan Kabot, Ed.D., CCC-SLP, and
Christine Reeve, Ph.D., BCBA-D

Foreword by L. Juane Heflin, Ph.D.

© 2010 AAPC
P.O. Box 23173
Shawnee Mission, Kansas 66283-0173
www.aapcpublishing.net

Publisher's Cataloging-in-Publication

Kabot, Susan.

Setting up classroom spaces that support students with autism spectrum disorders / Susan Kabot and Christine Reeve ; foreword by Juane Heflin. -- 1st ed. -- Shawnee Mission, Kan. : Autism Asperger Pub. Co., c2010.

p. ; cm.
ISBN: 978-1-934575-68-0
Includes bibliographical references.

1. Classrooms--Planning. 2. Classroom environment--Planning. 3. School facilities--Planning. 4. Schools--Furniture, equipment, etc.--Planning. 5. Autistic children--Education. 6. Autism spectrum disorders--Treatment. 7. Learning, Psychology of. 8. Spatial behavior. I. Reeve, Christine E. II. Title.

LB3325.C5 K33 2010   2010933011
371.6/21--dc22   1009

This book is designed in Sans Culottes and Calibri.

Printed in the United States of America.

Dedication

As so often happens in the field of autism spectrum disorders, professionals are attracted to the field from personal experience. In our case, Susan was pursuing her career as a special educator when her second son was diagnosed with autism. Christine grew up with an older sister with autism, although it was not diagnosed as such at the time. Given the impact that these experiences have had on us as professionals, we dedicate this book to Michael and Cathy, who remain our strongest influences.

Acknowledgments

We would like to thank the many teachers and administrators who have welcomed us into their schools and allowed us to photograph their classroom spaces and materials. We hope that by sharing their work with others through this book, their creativity and hard work will be expanded to help others educating students with autism.

We would also like to thank our families for their timeless support and patience as we travel across the country working with educational staff, families, and students with autism spectrum disorders. In addition, we would like to thank Brenda Myles for her support and insistence that this book be written, and Kirsten McBride for her assistance and guidance along the way.

TABLE OF CONTENTS

FOREWORD

In a shocking report, Kozol (1991) described the tragic outcomes of educating students in unacceptable school environments. Typically developing children attending overcrowded and dilapidated schools demonstrated poor academic achievement, high dropout rates, and rare entry into college.

Now imagine the anticipated outcomes for students whose neurology scrambles and shuffles relevant and irrelevant information and whose sensory systems make sustained focus difficult. Indeed, students with autism spectrum disorders (ASD) may feel stressed even in environments that neurotypical students would find ideal (Zentall & Zentall, 1983). Kanner (1943, p. 245) spoke of surroundings when he observed that children with autism could be driven to "despair" by aspects of their environments.

Unless the educational environment is designed to accommodate their unique learning characteristics, students with ASD will be stymied in their attempts to engage with their environments (Dunlap & Robbins, 1991), which will negatively affect their learning. In developing TEACCH (**T**reatment and **E**ducation of **A**utistic and **C**ommunication related handicapped **Ch**ildren), the first statewide intervention model for students with autism, Schopler, Brehm, Kinsbourne, and Reichler (1971) emphasized the importance of carefully engineering the physical and temporal parameters of classroom environments.

Students with ASD deserve practitioners who devote the time and energy necessary to construct environments, schedules, cueing systems, and engaging materials (Heflin & Alberto, 2001) to provide a platform for learning. The importance of establishing an educational environment conducive to learning has been reiterated in numerous reports and reviews. For example, Rogers (1999) noted that support for the hallmark characteristics of ASD is best addressed through environmental modifications and accommodations. Consideration needs to be given to the sensory differences experienced by many individuals with ASD or their learning will be inhibited (Duker & Rasing, 1989). More recently, the National Research Council (2001) described the value of supportive environments for students with ASD. Further, Iovanne, Dunlap, Huber, and Kincaid (2003) stated:

> A comprehensible classroom for students with ASD is one that is arranged in such a
> way as to elicit, facilitate, enhance, or support the acquisition of specific skills such

as language acquisition, appropriate behavior, social interactions, and targeted academic goals. (p. 158)

The National Autism Center, in the long-awaited National Standards Report of evidence-based practices for students with ASD (Wilczynski & Pollack, 2009), noted that antecedent modifications, such as environmental enrichment and environmental modification, are "established" interventions that have the weight of science to support their use.

In this much-needed book, Drs. Kabot and Reeve have created a concise guide of practical ideas that can be implemented immediately to create classroom environments that facilitate learning among students with ASD. Those of us who have been teachers can relate to the experiences of the fictional Ms. Gomez and Ms. Wilson, who serve as our tour guides, starting with the terror associated with being shown to a classroom of miscellaneous furniture and told "Good luck!" Even the helpful promise "tell me what you need and I'll order it" is worthless without ideas from those who have a global understanding of designing environments that promote engagement. Kabot and Reeve have that global understanding and provide clear rationales for the evidence-based practices they describe. Numerous photos are used to illustrate the critical concepts described in the narrative with sufficient variety so that teachers can accommodate a range of student needs and ages.

Kabot and Reeve do not abandon readers after enabling them to support the students they care about. That is, while their emphasis is on proactive strategies, the authors also provide important problem-solving ideas by analyzing the "warning signs" students give if more support is needed. Finally, the FAQs at the end of the book offer targeted solutions for specific situations that will be familiar to many who have experienced the joys and the challenges of working with students with ASD.

With few words and many illustrations, Kabot and Reeve "walk the talk" by depicting the educational structures that are necessary for students with ASD to be successful across all learning environments. Kozol sounded the alarm about the deleterious effects of substandard school environments for typically developing students. Kabot and Reeve raise an equivalent rallying call as they urge practitioners to design environments to engage students with ASD in learning and school communities to promote the highest levels of independence and productivity in these students' educational endeavors.

L. Juane Heflin, Ph.D.
Georgia State University

References

Duker, P. C., & Rasing, E. (1989). Effects of redesigning the physical environment and on-task behavior in three autistic-type developmentally disabled individuals. *Journal of Autism and Other Developmental Disorders, 19*, 449-60.

Dunlap, G., & Robbins, F. R. (1991). Current perspectives in service delivery for young children with autism. *Comprehensive Mental Health Care, 1,* 177-194.

Heflin, L. J., & Alberto, P. A. (2001). Establishing a behavioral context for learning with students with autism. *Focus on Autism & Other Developmental Disabilities, 16,* 93-101.

Iovannone, R., Dunlap, G., Huber, H., & Kincaid, D. (2003). Effective educational practices for students with autism spectrum disorders. *Focus on Autism and Other Developmental Disabilities, 18*, 150-165.

Kanner, L. (1943). Autistic disturbances of affective contact. *The Nervous Child, 2,* 217-250.

Kozol, J. (1991). *Savage inequalities: Children in America's schools.* New York: Harper Collins.

National Research Council. (2001). *Educating children with autism.* Committee on Educational Interventions for Children with Autism. Division of Behavioral and Social Sciences and Education. Washington, DC: National Academy Press.

Rogers, S. J. (1999). Intervention for young children with autism: From research to practice. *Infants and Young Children, 12*(2), 1-16.

Schopler, E., Brehm, S., Kinsbourne, M., & Reichler, R. J. (1971). The effect of treatment structure on development of autistic children. *Archives of General Psychiatry, 24*, 415-421.

Wilczynski, S. M., & Pollack, E. G. (Eds.). (2009). *Evidence-based practice and autism in the schools: A guide to providing appropriate interventions to students with autism spectrum disorders.* Randolph, MA: National Autism Center.

Zentall, S. S., & Zentall T. R. (1983). Optimal stimulation: A model of disordered activity and performance in normal and deviant children. *Psychological Bulletin, 94,* 446-471.

INTRODUCTION

THE INFLUENCE OF THE PHYSICAL ENVIRONMENT ON STUDENT BEHAVIOR

Ms. Wilson is a teacher in a self-contained classroom for students with autism spectrum disorders (ASD). This year she is expecting to teach eight students and is beginning in a new room. Her principal has given her two days to set up her classroom. When she walked into the room one week before the start of school, she found two large kidney-shaped tables, three student desks, and three teacher desks in addition to a computer table, a file cabinet, built-in shelves and a closet, and a timeout area. Her principal told her she could look in the storage areas for additional furniture if needed, but he did not know what type of furniture might be available.

Ms. Wilson is concerned about how she is going to set up a classroom that can meet the needs of her students and is not sure about where to begin.

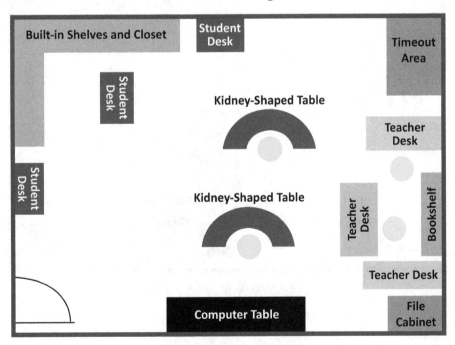

Ms. Wilson's "before" classroom layout.

Ms. Gomez is a teacher with 20 years of experience in special education, but she has never had a class that is as challenging as the one she is teaching this year. Her current classroom is comprised of three students with ASD and eight students with learning disability or behavior disorder eligibilities. Since the start of the school year, Ms. Gomez has had difficulty getting the class settled into instruction during the school day. Dontel, one of the students with ASD, constantly runs around the room. His favorite activity is running around the rectangular table in the center of the classroom. Jarmaine likes to climb on the furniture and jump from shelf to shelf. The other students have difficulty staying in their seats during all of this activity and are constantly laughing and wandering away from instruction to see what is going on in other parts of the room. The majority of work is done at the two rectangular tables with the full group, in the middle of the class, and there is limited time in the schedule for breaking into smaller groups for more direct instruction.

Ms. Gomez has been trying to make do with the materials and the furniture that the previous teacher left, but some of her materials are incomplete or in disrepair, and for some students she is even lacking materials to meet their IEP goals. The classroom has a variety of shelves and closets, but they are fixed and cannot be moved. Her principal felt that she needed fewer shelves for the middle of the classroom despite her request. As a result, she has limited furniture to provide boundaries for students to understand the limits of the space of their work areas.

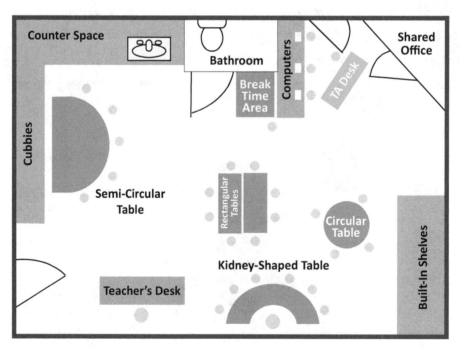

Ms. Gomez's "before" classroom layout.

Ms. Gomez has two rectangular tables put together as one, a small round table, a semi-circle table that is rarely used, a teacher and a teacher assistant's (TA) desks, and a built-in shelf for computers. Her room backs up against an office that she shares with the teacher next door, which is not used for students.

The Impact of the Characteristics of Autism and the Physical Environment

The characteristics of students with ASD have a significant impact on their learning style and ability to learn in classroom environments. For instance, students with ASD often have difficulty making independent transitions to new activities due to their lack of understanding of nonverbal cues and anxiety surrounding new situations. Establishing visual cues and schedules within the classroom can help them make transitions with a minimum of challenging behavior.

In addition, students with ASD often have attention and sensory needs that impact their ability to focus on the main speaker in the classroom due to distractions, or they are unable to isolate relevant and meaningful information from classroom activities or materials from everything else that is going on around them. Well-organized classrooms seek to manage these challenges and minimize the impact that they have on the learning of students with ASD by providing clear cues and structure to the room.

The list on page 8 highlights the major characteristics of ASD and areas where they dictate the need for support in the classroom via structure and organization.

Characteristics of Autism Spectrum Disorders
That Dictate the Need for Structure and Organization

Characteristics	Physical Space	Materials	Visual Cues
Social			
Uses poor eye contact or fails to orient to others	X		
Has difficulty maintaining personal space, physically intrudes on others			X
Has difficulty taking turns in social interactions or activities		X	X
Has difficulty joining an activity	X	X	
Has difficulty waiting	X		X
Shows little curiosity or interest in others or the immediate environment – appears to be in "own world"		X	
Restricted Patterns of Behavior, Interests, and Activities			
Expresses strong need for routine or "sameness" – has difficulty with change			X
Uses objects in repetitive, atypical manner (e.g., meticulously lines up objects, purposefully drops objects to see them fall)		X	X
Has difficulty transitioning from a preferred activity	X		X
Has strong need for closure or difficulty stopping a task before it is completed			X
Displays difficulty engaging in activities other than intense special interests		X	X
Communication			
Has difficulty expressing wants and needs		X	X
Has difficulty following instructions	X	X	X
Displays little pretend or imaginative play or thought		X	
Gives false impression of understanding more than he/she actually does			X
Sensory Differences			
Responds in an unusual manner to sounds (e.g., ignores sounds or over-reacts to sudden, unexpected noises, high-pitched continuous sounds, or complex/multiple noises)	X		
Responds in an unusual manner to light or color (e.g., focuses on shiny items, shadows, reflections, shows preference or strong dislike for certain colors)	X		
Cognitive Differences			
Has attention problems	X	X	X
Has difficulty organizing self in order to initiate or complete an activity		X	X
Has poor organizational skills	X	X	X
Motor Differences			
Has poor motor coordination or is accident prone	X		X
Has difficulty moving through environment (e.g., in and out of buildings, using stairs, walking on uneven surfaces)	X		
Emotional Vulnerability			
Is anxious or easily stressed (worries obsessively)	X		X
Exhibits rage reactions or "meltdowns" in response to apparently minor events			X
Has difficulty managing stress and/or anxiety	X		X

Note. Characteristics represent a partial list from the *Underlying Characteristics Checklist – High-Functioning* and *Underlying Characteristics Checklist – Classic* by Ruth Aspy and Barry G. Grossman. Available from www.asperger.net.

Clear visual cues and the use of furniture as boundaries for learning areas help all students to focus on the task of learning rather than having to concentrate on navigating the environment. The classroom with poorly arranged furniture can encourage running in open areas, climbing on the furniture, and downtime caused by the teacher having to redirect students to the necessary areas. Lack of functional visual cues within the room fails to give students and staff information about where they are expected to work, what materials they are to use, and how to clean up successfully when an activity ends.

Careful attention must be paid to the arrangement of the furniture, placement and use of visual cues like schedules and labels of items, the flow of traffic throughout the classroom, and the placement of materials in the learning environment to provide information to the students about what is going to take place and what behaviors are expected. As in any classroom, creating a safe environment is of upmost importance. In classrooms for students with ASD, it is important to remember this through all age levels, as even older students may not anticipate dangerous situations. For example, students may put small objects in their mouths and accidentally swallow them while working with manipulatives for an activity. These students may also not be able to communicate that they have stepped in an ant bed and have ants from the playground in their shoes and socks.

Goals of Organizing the Physical Environment

The primary goal of designing classroom space is to make sure that the room promotes engagement in instruction throughout the day. Several elements combine to create an environment in which students have limited downtime and clearly understand what they are expected to do in each area of the classroom, all to ensure the best possible learning outcomes, both short and long term.

A well-organized classroom meets the following criteria:

- Creates an environment with predictability and stability to enhance skill acquisition and facilitate participation in activities
- Sets up areas of the classroom based on the needs of the students and the classroom space
- Develops clearly defined areas of an appropriate size for a given activity
- Gives clear cues to students and staff about expectations for different areas of the room (e.g., a set of chairs set in a circle around the instructor gives a cue that students are expected to sit in a group and attend to the leader of the group)
- Allows supervision of all students within the classroom (e.g., having low shelves that allow the teacher to observe other students in the classroom from her work area with a small group of students ensures that all the students are supervised and none are behind barriers where they cannot be seen by the teacher)

- Creates classroom areas that support the targeted skills for scheduled activities
- Develops areas that limit distractions and help students focus on the task at hand
- Creates environments that increase engagement and prevent challenging behaviors
- Fosters student independence in navigating the classroom routine and everyday activities
- Creates work spaces to promote engagement in the general education classroom, as sometimes the general education classroom can be overwhelming to students with ASD

What You Will Find in This Book

In order to meet the above goals and criteria for well-designed classrooms, this book will look at the typical areas of the classroom and present suggestions and strategies for providing visual supports, clear boundaries using furniture and other materials, and methods of organizing materials that support the learning of students with ASD.

This book is designed to help both Ms. Wilson and Ms. Gomez depicted at the beginning of this chapter, and many other teachers, to determine what type of furniture and materials they need and how to arrange them in a way that creates an effective learning environment and prevents problem behaviors. Specifically, the book will

- examine the goals of organizing the physical environment
- outline the typical areas of classrooms and the elements to consider in designing them
- examine what to take into consideration when acquiring and organizing classroom materials
- list resources that can assist in acquiring appropriate materials for the classroom design and developing visual cues to support learning, along with applications and examples of these design elements

Throughout, the specific needs of students with ASD will underlie the discussion and will be illustrated though various classroom scenarios and lots of photos of real students in real classrooms.

THE ELEMENTS OF A TYPICAL CLASSROOM

For many teachers, their classroom changes every year. Often this is because of the different needs of their students, which demand a different physical environment, schedule, and set of strategies. Nevertheless, although the specific activities and lesson plans may change from year to year, several areas remain stable in classroom environments. These include areas for

- one-to-one instruction
- small-group instruction
- independent work
- full-group instruction
- computer or media-related activities
- transition
- cool-down or sensory space
- a teacher place for administrative functions

In the following, we will look at each of these areas and discuss their function and how they can best be set up to meet the needs of students with ASD. Examples across grade levels are given.

One-to-One Instruction Area

Many students, particularly at young ages, benefit from one-to-one instruction. This may be an appropriate place for providing highly individualized instruction like discrete trial training or for any type of instruction for a student who is highly distractible in other environments. Such instruction commonly focuses on learning readiness skills such as attending to adults and following directions. In addition, it can help prepare students for group instruction.

Not all students require a one-to-one teaching area; therefore, not all classrooms include such a dedicated space. Some students are able to learn within small groups of two or three students. However, if needed, this area would be comprised of a small desk or table and a chair each for the adult and the child. In a preschool or early-elementary classroom, the adult's chair should be child-sized to allow the adult to be at eye level with the student. If the child is just learning to remain in his or her seat, the furniture may be arranged to give clear physical boundaries to the area and help the student remain within the work space.

A student participating in 1-1 discrete trial training. In this picture, the student is sitting with his back to a divider in the room and facing the instructor. The instructor is sitting on the floor so as to be at the child's eye level to present instructions. An Educube and Edutray (see Classroom Supply List) are used to establish clear boundaries for the child to remain in his seat. The tray provides a work surface that the instructor can easily reach across and gives the student the cue that he needs to remain in his seat, yet it is simply resting on the arms of the chair so that if he stands up, it will fall away (i.e., it is not restraining him in his seat).

A 1-1 communication lesson. This picture illustrates how the Edutray rests on the arms of the Educube. This teacher is sitting in a child-sized chair close to the child's so she can facilitate a communicative exchange using the Picture Exchange Communication System (PECS). The student's back is to a bookshelf, providing a clear boundary behind him. In front of him is another bookshelf to block distractions from other areas of the room.

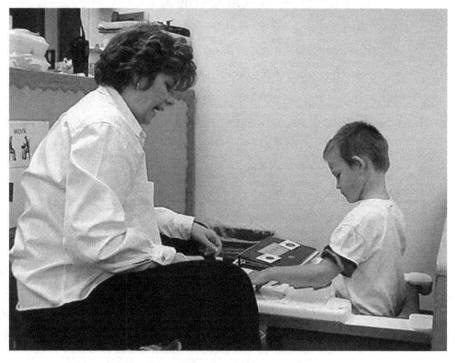

Small-Group Instruction Area

Most classrooms also include an area where students can work in small groups. Students may rotate through these areas, such as a center rotation for kindergarteners, or they may choose from various activities that take place in these areas. Within these spaces, students may work together or directly with the instructor on targeted activities.

The structure of the area depends on the type of activity expected to take place. For instance, in preschool or kindergarten classrooms, play is often a small-group activity and takes place in an area surrounded by shelves of toys that are easily accessible at the children's level and typically include housekeeping furniture like a play kitchen. The shelves and housekeeping furniture also serve to provide boundaries for the play area.

Play area for young children with play kitchen. The bookshelves provide a clear definition of the size of the play kitchen area, while also serving to store materials for various types of play.

Preschool play area with a small picnic table in the center. The shelves provide boundaries to keep students and the materials for the play area contained within the space. The shelves also serve to store materials.

Play area for pretend play in preschool with a smaller table with two chairs to accompany the kitchen area. Shelves separate the play area from the transition area nearby while also providing storage for play materials.

For table-based activities like art, games, or academics, tables may be arranged to limit distractibility by having the students face away from the rest of the classroom. This arrangement also allows the instructor to supervise outside this area.

Reading area for small-group instruction. Students are facing the wall so that they are not distracted by other activities going on in the room at the same time.

Tables may also be arranged so that the students sit between the table and the wall to prevent them from leaving the area.

Small-group instruction area in a preschool class. One of the tables is turned to prevent students from leaving the area.

The furniture may also be set up to facilitate collaborative group work by arranging desks in pods where four or five students face each other while sitting in their group.

First-grade classroom with desks arranged in small groups.

Arranging the desks so that students face each other in small groups facilitates social interaction and collaboration and offers opportunities for peer support for the student with ASD. Students are attending to each other so that they can work together on group projects, and it is easy for a child who needs extra assistance to look at the materials (e.g., books) of the other students for cues about what to do next.

Small-group work area for 18- to 22-year-olds working on vocational activities.

Small-group area in an elementary classroom with furniture set to create clear boundaries.

Small-group work area where the students face away from other activities in the classroom. Work materials are stored in the shelves to the right of the teacher.

An area for looking at books in the preschool classroom. The seating area serves as the boundary with an area rug to define the space.

This table is set up for social skills lessons with preschoolers. It is low to the ground, so the children sit on the floor; it is set up with visuals for turn taking and requesting. The beanbags are used to pass to students as a way to indicate whose turn it is in a game or a conversation. The children face the shelves to limit distractions from the rest of the room.

Direct-instruction area for preschool. The students sit in Educubes (see Classroom Supply List) with trays to facilitate working with the teacher and provide boundaries for where to sit and work. The teacher sits in a child-size chair to be at the children's level during instruction.

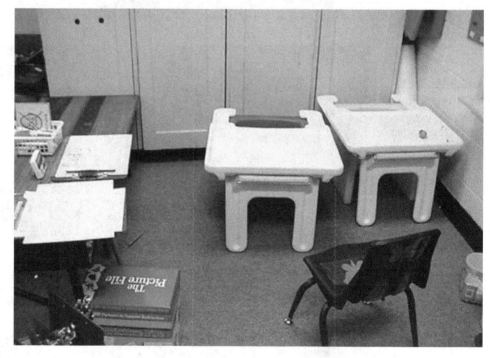

Independent Work Area

These are areas of the classroom in which the student learns to work on his own to practice mastered skills without additional assistance from adults. For children who are included in the general education environment, this area may be their desks or a more secluded area that allows for reduced distractions. To minimize distractions, in these areas the student typically faces away from the activity of the classroom, often toward a wall or other barrier such as a bookshelf or divider.

Some students benefit from the use of study carrels for this type of activity to help them to concentrate on the task at hand. Since an instructor is not working directly with the student, there may be enough space for an adult to stand behind the student (to prompt as needed through the task), but there must be easy access for the adult to fade out of the area to encourage independence. Tasks in this area must be visually cued, clear, and organized to ensure that the student knows what is expected and when the work is completed.

Independent work systems are part of structured teaching, as defined by the TEACCH (Treatment and Education of Autistic and related Communication-handicapped Children) program. They are designed to teach students to work independently given a specific structured system with visual cues. (More information may be found at http://www.teacch.com.)

Work systems typically have a built-in schedule that indicates the work that is expected of the student, a defined set of materials that indicate how much work is expected, tasks that are clearly defined for the students regarding how to complete the task, and information on the schedule regarding what the student should do when he or she is finished.

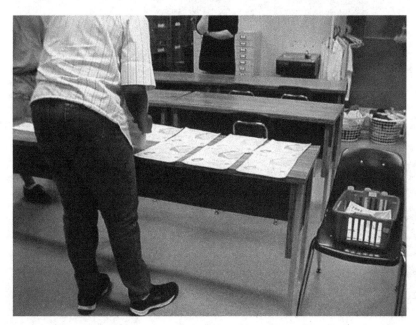

A high school student is collating documents on a table with visual cues of pages numbered to lay out the task and the finished products in a basket on the chair to the right. The left-to-right setup of the system, with visual cues on the table telling the student where to set up the pages, helps the student to complete this task independently.

A middle school independent work system with the tasks stacked in boxes in front of the students.

Students working on independent work. The numbers on the work baskets indicate the task from their schedule that they picked up and brought to the table.

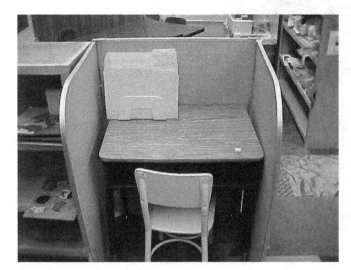

Independent work station that includes a carrel to prevent distraction from other activities in the room. The students can complete work from the tasks in the folders and place their completed work in an inbox kept on the desk or the floor to the right.

Two independent work systems are set up so that students can learn to take work from the shelf on the left, complete it, and put it in the "finished" baskets on the floor. The tables face the wall to prevent distraction.

This work area faces a divider as a barrier to prevent distraction.

Two work systems at one table for preschoolers. Two students sit beside each other and work from their schedule on the left to the "finished" basket on the right. Two work systems are set up, one in front of each chair with corresponding finished baskets on the right. This allows a larger table to be used to accommodate two work systems. Students face the wall and windows with closed blinds to prevent distractions from other activities in the room or outside.

High school student doing an assembly task in a carrel as part of an independent work system.

Some work systems include fewer baskets to meet the individual needs of the students. For a student who is unable to independently complete a series of tasks, work systems may be set up with one or two baskets, with the schedule modified accordingly, to shape independence. As the student is able to independently complete two baskets, a third can be added. Task complexity, amount of materials in the tasks, and the number of tasks can be increased as the student becomes more proficient at working independently.

Tape provides boundaries on this table set up for two independent work systems. They also include picture/symbols for the student to communicate for assistance, attention, and a break.

Full-Group Table Activities

In all types of classrooms, some activities require classroom meetings at a table or desks, with a surface for the students to work on. In general education, activities of full-group instruction typically take place at a group of student desks. In self-contained settings, the number of students in a full-group activity usually ranges between 5 and 12 and can be accommodated at one large table.

Sometimes teachers have no choice about the type or size of the table available in the classroom, but ideally the table should be chosen based on the number of students who will use it simultaneously and the type of activity in which they will be engaging.

A kidney-shaped table is ideal for activities that require the students to focus on a central instructor or communicative partner. This type of setup is excellent for activities that involve communication and participation since all of the students can see each other, the materials can be stored in the middle of the table for ready access, and the instructor can easily reach the materials and each student for assistance as needed.

Kidney-shaped large-group table serves as the morning meeting area with the schedules and calendar on the wall behind it.

At this kidney-shaped table, students return from the playground to snack, with the snack materials set out so that the students can immediately sit down and engage in the activity. Chairs are Educubes (see Classroom Supply List).

In this arrangement, preschool students can all face and reach the teacher for a full-group activity, such as snack. (The pockets on the back of the chairs allow for storage of communication systems and other material that may be helpful for the student in the activity but would clutter the table.)

Students' names on the table indicate where the students are to sit, with color cues that match their schedule color.

A large rectangular or circular table can be useful for activities such as games or art activities that are completed in larger groups where there is no designated leader. The table should always be large enough to accommodate everyone comfortably without crowding. If a large enough table is not available, two or more tables may be pushed together in a V shape, a U shape, or doubled to make a square or rectangle in order to accommodate all the students.

In general education classrooms, when there is a 1:1 paraprofessional, it is often useful to have a rolling stool so that the aide can move in and out to prompt only when necessary.

This group table was created by putting together three trapezoid tables in a resource classroom to accommodate group work.

If no tables are available in the classroom, individual desks may be arranged to create a group area by placing them in a U or a square, dependent upon the activity that is to occur.

Full-Group Open Area

Some activities in the classroom schedule require students to meet without needing a table or work surface. Such activities may involve young children sitting on the carpet for storytime, older students engaging in an exercise routine, or elementary students meeting for a morning calendar program to start their day.

Despite the need for more open space in this type of activity, it is critical to have boundaries and structure to give students information about where to stand or sit and where to focus their attention. Dependent upon the type of activity, chairs may be set up in a circle so the students can sit facing the instructor. Many teachers find it useful to have rolling stools available for the adults so that they can move closer and fade back quickly and easily during instruction.

This group meeting area uses chairs to outline the space and distance from the teacher.

In this preschool classroom, the students sit in Educubes (see Classroom Supply List) to define the boundaries between them. The teacher sits on a rolling stool when conducting circle so she can move close to individual children with visual supports and then move back to address the whole class.

Transition Area

Due to their desire for routine and sameness and their difficulty with shifting attention between tasks, many students with ASD struggle with transitions.

Transitions can involve ...

- switching between tasks but remaining in the same area
- switching between areas within the classroom
- transitioning to and from the classroom for a variety of activities or classes (e.g., recess, lunch, P.E.)

To assist with transitions that involve movement within or outside the classroom, the use of transition strategies (such as hand signals, music) and establishing areas of the classroom where students go to check their schedule or get information about transitions provide predictability. The student goes to that area of the room when the transition signal is given (e.g., bell ringing, teacher direction).

Students with ASD inherently benefit from visual strategies such as visual schedules, including objects, photos, picture icons, and written schedules, depending on their skill levels. More information about the use of schedules may be found in Chapter 4 and at http://www.teacch.com/. The transition area in the classroom is a consistent place such as near the door or in a corner, where the students may check their schedules or assemble to wait for a transition to occur.

In general education settings, particularly at younger ages, students line up at the door before proceeding to other parts of the school. A student with ASD may have a schedule in his or her binder or desk that gives information about when and where to line up for the next activity.

In self-contained settings, students may have a visual daily schedule that is located on the wall in a transition area of the classroom. This space contains each student's schedule and serves as the gathering place for students to wait or check their schedules before moving to the next activity.

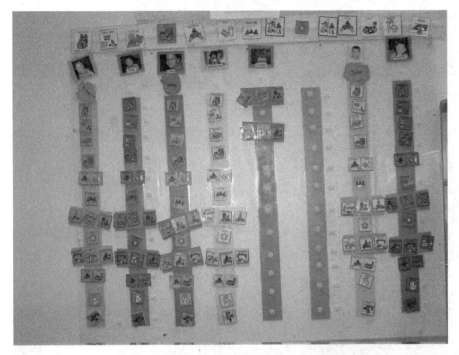

Individual schedules for pre-school students using cross-bars for center rotations that allow for the full-day schedule to fit on the wall.

Individual schedules on the wall. The students turn over the visuals when they check them to indicate the next activity when they return.

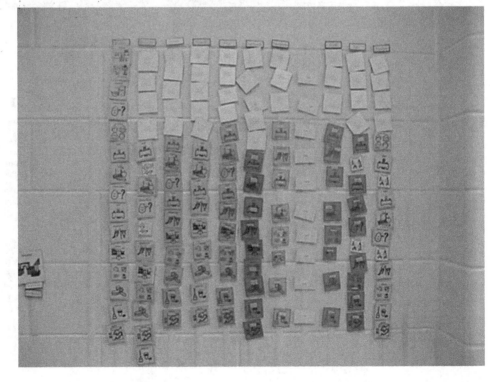

In this middle school classroom, students need a variety of schedules. This transition area includes picture schedules, written schedules, and a first-then schedule. (First-then schedules are designed for students who may become overwhelmed with a full-day schedule that shows all the activities and benefit from a schedule that just presents what they are doing now and what they will do next.)

In this classroom, several students need object schedules. This transition area includes their object schedules. The object schedules are constructed by finding objects representative of the activity and gluing them to a piece of matte board and labeling them. The label helps the staff remember the representative meaning of the object.

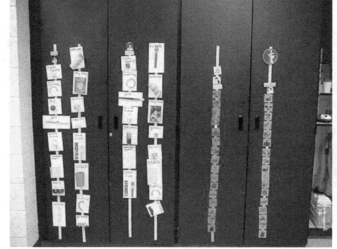

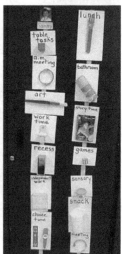

In this classroom, the transition area has cubbies for storing the children's coats and materials.

This transition area is in the hallway for children to store coats, boots, and belongings to avoid cluttering the classroom.

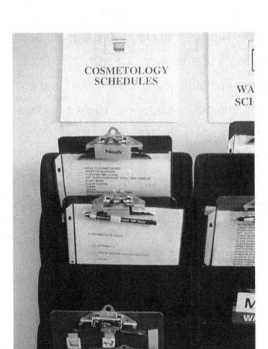

This transition area stores written schedules for high school students to complete jobs at job sites.

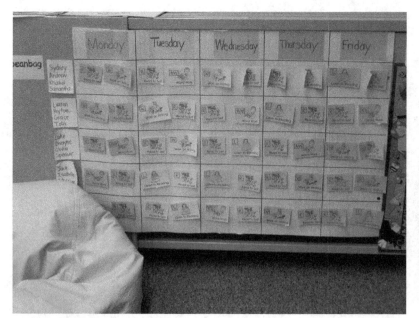

This is the center rotation schedule for a general education first-grade class that includes a student with ASD. The pictures under each day represent the centers for the day, while the names to the left refer to groups of students.

Cool-Down or Sensory Area

Many students with ASD have difficulty regulating sensory input and may become overwhelmed by common classroom activities such as loud music during exercise time or the noise and smell of the cafeteria. Sensory overload often leads to meltdowns that can derail the student's ability to focus on the curricular activities of the day.

To prevent these types of behavior, many students benefit from a cool-down or sensory area in the classroom where they can temporarily escape from the general classroom activity and engage in activities that have a calming effect. For some students this may include soft lighting or soothing music, for others it may include the use of fidget toys like slinkies or items with visual effects like kaleidoscopes or glitter wands. Some students need an enclosed space in the room like a tent while others are fine with a table or desk where calming materials are available.

Regardless of the form of the area, it is critical that the sensory area be used to help prevent problem behaviors and not as a consequence for those behaviors. In other words, the area should not double as a time-out area or be used to separate the student from the group. Time in the sensory area should be voluntary and have a beneficial effect for the student to be successful.

(Left) This cool-down area is designed for a class of children with a variety of disabilities, including ASD. Cloth hung from the ceiling, lava lamps, and light strings offer a quiet, calming area along with a variety of sensory toys and activities.

(Below) This visual is placed in a cool-down area to help students remember how to calm down when upset or angry.

This tent in a preschool classroom is designed to provide a reading area that is calming and set off from the activities of the room.

Computer and Media Area

Most classrooms today are equipped with one or more computers and other types of media equipment such as card readers, tape recorders, and other independent electronic learning devices. Such devices can be grouped together in a media center that can include such activities as working on the computer, practicing spelling words by recording them on the card reader, listening to books on tape or CD, or reviewing and maintaining skills using the computer.

These devices require proximity to power outlets, which must be considered when arranging the room. Frequently, power outlets are limited in classrooms. As a result, placement of electronic devices often serves as the first element of the room design. In other words, the media center's place in the classroom may be fixed and the rest of the areas may have to be arranged around it.

Desks and tables serve as good structures for this type of equipment, but care should be taken to stow away power cords and access to electrical sockets, particularly in rooms with young children. Outlet covers must be placed on all unused electric outlets. It is recommended that computers be placed with their backs against a wall or some barrier to prevent students from becoming entangled in, or playing with, the electrical cords. Bins and baskets can be used to store media for the equipment such as tapes, CDs, and cartridges. These may be placed in easy reach for students who are expected to use the center independently or out of reach for students who are working on making requests for desired items.

Two students can take turns using the computer in this computer center. The furniture is sized for young children to sit comfortably.

This classroom has a media center in which the teacher has separated the functions of two computers. One computer is labeled for computer work and the other is designated for computer fun. This allows the students to understand when it is appropriate to play games and when it is time to work.

This listening center has a card reader for students to practice articulation, vocabulary, and personal information. The visual for the card reader indicates the directions students are to follow independently to complete the task of listening to the recorded words and writing them down.

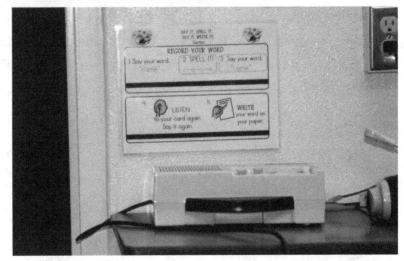

Administration/Teacher Area

In general education classrooms, the teacher has a desk that is often at the front of the classroom. In some cases, the teacher sets her desk off to the side to prevent it from being the center of attention. This is important, because the most effective teaching strategies indicate that it is important that teachers move about the classroom while teaching to prevent disruptive behavior through proximity control and to be able to continually assess students' engagement and understanding of the material.

In nontraditional and self-contained classrooms, the teacher's desk often serves primarily as a storage area during the school day and as a work area for the teacher after the students leave. Further, in many classrooms for students with ASD, other professionals in addition to the teacher work in the room and need a place to store personal belongings and access to a work surface.

Considerations for Design and Placement of the Administration Area

1. **Given the amount of space available for working with students in the room, determine how much space can be afforded to staff areas.** In small classrooms, teachers and paraprofessionals may share one desk or eliminate the administrative desk in order to create more space for working with the students.

2. **Carefully plan for the privacy of the administration area.** Confidential documents must be kept in a locked cabinet. Similarly, grade books, IEP documents, and other materials should not be left out where students might see them. Therefore, administration areas should include a locked storage unit for confidential information. This unit may also double as a secure area to place personal items such as purses to prevent theft.

3. **Determine which parts of the administration area the students should have access to.** For instance, students may need to access an inbox on the teacher's desk in order to turn in assignments. However, students should not have access to the teacher's grade book at the same time. These areas should be clearly marked with signs or other visual cues so the students are clearly aware of what they are allowed to touch and what is off limits.

This teacher has her lesson plans open on her desk for easy access. This allows substitutes and teacher aides to know what is supposed to happen during the day if the teacher is not available.

Summary

It is important to consider the learning characteristics of students with ASD when designing classroom environments. Each group of students will require different levels of support from the arrangement of the classroom. The instructional areas in the classroom must meet the curriculum needs of each student as well as the class as a whole. Care should be taken to clearly identify areas by their function and indicate the expected behavior of the students while working there.

CHAPTER 2

DESIGNING AREAS OF THE CLASSROOM

Once the areas needed in the classroom have been determined as part of the academic schedule, certain considerations must be addresses to ensure that students with ASD can focus on the activities that occur in each area.

Guidelines for Room Design

1. **Make sure each area of the room is functional for the activity that will be taking place.** Activities that involve movement should occur in larger spaces; those that are sedentary will require less space. If an activity requires a lot of materials (e.g., individualized instruction for each child targeting unique IEP goals), make sure that there is enough storage available nearby. Conduct activities that require electricity near outlets. Place activities that require water for the activity itself or for cleanup near a water source if there is one in the room. Such activities may include art, sensory, science, snack, and mealtimes.

2. **Assign areas in the classroom so that children are not distracted by neighboring activities when they are doing work that requires concentration**. For example, noisy activities like playing games and playing with pretend play toys should not occur next to direct instruction in preacademic or academic subjects. Similarly, if students are distracted by the computer, do not place the computer next to a work area where students need to attend to instruction or work independently.

3. **Define each area by clear boundaries.** Boundaries may be created by the use of walls, furniture, or dividers. Shelving units are useful for dividing areas as well as organizing and storing the materials and equipment necessary for the activities that will take place in a given area. Hinged storage units also work well to provide boundaries that can be changed or moved.

This play area is defined by storage units that hold the material for a given activity. Note the hinged cabinet that is closed in the bottom of the area. It can be opened when students are in the area and need access to the toys.

In this classroom, the furniture makes two separate areas for different activities to take place in. On one side of the bookshelves is a library area with beanbags for seating. On the other is a direct-instruction area with materials for teaching in labeled bins underneath the curtains.

4. **Maintain adult supervision of each area.** Depending upon the number of staff assigned to the room and the number of activities that are taking place simultaneously, area boundaries should be low enough so that the adult has a clear view of the students in each area.

The low shelves here ensure that the teaching staff is able to monitor students in any area of the room.

5. **Help students differentiate the functions of areas of the classroom when different activities take place in the same space at different times during the day.** Provide a cue to students so they know what will be occurring at each of those times. For example, the large-group table may be used for snack midmorning and for art in the afternoon. In that case, placemats might be used when the students are having snacks to differentiate it from art time. In other cases, you might change the label of the area, place a different picture for the students to check, or use a tablecloth or similar material to change the look of the area.

This picture shows a large-group table that is used for cooking and art and at other times is set up with placemats to indicate that it is time for snack. The placemats are place setting templates that one of the students uses to set the table for snack.

6. **Consider the flow of traffic as students move between activities in the room.** This is especially important during center rotations when groups of children are moving at the same time between activities. Design the schedule so that groups of children are moving in either a clockwise or counterclockwise fashion. If there is a student in a wheelchair or students with limited mobility, make sure there is ample space for them to move in.

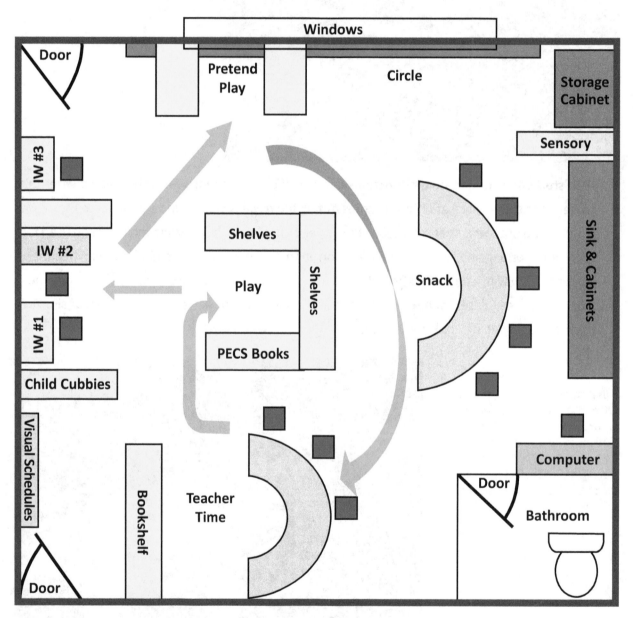

In this drawing, the green arrows demonstrate the flow of traffic from one center to the next in a preschool classroom. The students move from the teacher time (i.e., direct instruction) area, to the play area, to the independent work area, and finally to the pretend play area. IW = independent work area.

Examples of Floor Plans With Corresponding Schedules

It is important that the physical space and the instructional areas support the schedule of activities that occur each day. For example, if three activities are taking place at the same time during a center rotation (reading, game playing, and mathematics), three small-group instructional areas with a table and chairs are needed. In the following are sample floor plans with corresponding schedules that represent a resource classroom and a self-contained classroom. Each had different challenges in the design and different considerations for materials and furniture.

Ms. Wilson's "after" floor plan. On page 41, please note the "after" picture of Ms. Wilson's classroom (see "before" classroom layout on page 5). Remember that Ms. Wilson had very limited furniture in her room and was told she could look in the school storage closet for additional items if she needed them.

Given the austerity of her room in terms of furniture and materials, Ms. Wilson needed a significant number of shelves and dividers to help structure the space of her room. She was unable to find additional furniture in the storage rooms, but she approached somebody in the maintenance department in the school district who was willing to make her some simple wood structures. This allowed her to add four bookshelves and four dividers to provide boundaries for open areas and to create clear areas for different activities rather than having to rely on one or two large tables for the majority of the day.

For the morning rotation, students rotated systematically through center activities in staggered order – from individualized instruction to independent work, to reading, to math. The individualized instruction activity focused on specific IEP goals that were the reason why students attended the resource room (e.g., more math or reading, social skills).

For the students with ASD, instruction focused primarily on language and communication activities. In the afternoon, the class rotated through a set of leisure-based centers – from art to games, to computer. The computer table had to remain in the same area to access the power outlets, but since one of the students was highly distracted by the computer screens when he was involved in other activities, the computers were placed at the end of the long table with their screens angled toward the wall.

Ms. Wilson's Self-Contained Class Schedule

10 students, 3 staff

NAMES	J	R	AJ	JA	S	V	M	D	L	T
8:00-8:15	Table Tasks[1]									
8:15-8:30	Breakfast									
8:30-9:00	Group	Speech M/W	Group	Group	Group	Speech T/Th	Group	Group	Group	Group
9:00-9:20	Reading	Math	Indiv.	Reading	Reading	Indiv.	I.W.[3]	Math	I.W.	Math
9:20-9:40	Math	Indiv.	I.W.	Math	Math	I.W.	Reading	Indiv.	Reading	Indiv.
9:40-10:00		I.W.	Reading	Indiv.	Indiv.	Reading	Math	I.W.	Math	
10:00-10:10		Transition Group								
10:10-10:40		Social Skills	PE/Music	PE/Music	Social Skills	PE/Music	Social Skills	Social Skills		Social Skills
10:40-11:00		Reading	Math	I.W.		Math		Reading	D.I.	Reading
11-11:20			Choice	Choice		Choice		Choice	Choice	Choice
11:20-11:30			Hygiene	Hygiene		Hygiene		Hygiene		
11:30-12:05			Lunch	Lunch		Lunch				
12:05-12:15			Recess	Recess		Recess				
12:15-12:30	Table Tasks		Table Tasks	Table Tasks	Table Tasks	Table Tasks				Table Tasks
12:30-12:50	Comp.[4]		Art	Comp.	Comp.	Art	Games	Games		Games
12:50-1:10	Art		Games	Art	Art	Games	Comp.	Comp.		Comp.
1:10-1:30	Games	Games	Comp.	Speech	Games	Comp.	Art	Art		
1:30-1:45			Snack	Speech		Snack		Snack		
1:45-2:00			Pack-up	Speech		Pack-up		Pack-up		

[1]Table tasks can be visual motor tasks at the table or journals.

[2]Indiv. = Individualized instruction. Additional instruction or need for resource instruction.

[3]IW = Independent work based on structured teaching with a visually cued work system.

[4]Comp. = computer time.

Shaded areas indicate time student spend in the general education classroom.

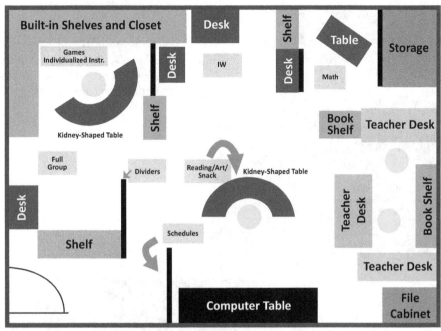

Ms. Wilson's "after" classroom layout.

This shows an individual student's independent work area. This student was highly distracted by other activities in the room. The teacher used a carrel to wall off the area to prevent distraction. The student worked from files in the folders on his left to put them in a "finished" box to the right of the cubby.

This is a more traditional independent work area in the same center area of the classroom. This was one of three work systems within the center for the room.

This is a wider shot of the full independent work area. The table in the forefront is the reading area; the individualized instruction, independent work, and math centers move from left to right.

This is the individualized instruction center. The students face the wall to prevent distractions from other activities in the room and to allow the teacher to look out and supervise the other students. Low shelves provide a boundary between this area and the independent work area (to the viewer's right), and the closet and shelves in the back allow storage for materials.

This is the math center of the morning rotation. The calendar and math manipulatives are stored here. On the front of the shelf that separates the math center from the rest of the room hang students' communication books and check-in envelopes for their schedules.

These are the individual schedules for the students in Ms. Wilson's self-contained room. They are placed in front of the door so they are the first thing the students see when they come in. Care was taken to place them away from the immediate doorway, however, to prevent traffic jams as the students enter the room. The divider on which they hang serves as a barrier to stop the students when they enter the room and to help them remember to check their schedule.

Ms. Gomez's "after" floor plan. While Ms. Gomez had a variety of built-in shelves and several tables in the room (see page 6), the students were spending the majority of their time at the center rectangular tables. Little instruction was going on at other tables. In addition, because of the built-in shelves, Ms. Gomez did not have any movable shelves to store materials where they were needed. Consequently, materials were not set up prior to the activity, so students had downtime while waiting for the teacher to gather materials from other parts of the room. The downtime led to students getting up and leaving the area when they were not engaged and taking materials from other students while waiting for their own work.

To address this concern, Ms. Gomez found shelves in one of the storage rooms in the school and used them to provide more definition of space and to store materials closer to where they were needed at the tables. The built-in shelves were useful for the independent work areas by serving to store the tasks to the left and continuing the left-to-right progression of the work systems. The students were facing the wall so that they were free from the distractions of the room.

The students rotated in the morning through reading, independent work, and math centers. In the afternoon, they were divided into two groups – an art activity and games – and then switched. After snack, they were again divided into two groups – language and social group – and then switched. The art and the social groups worked at the small-group tables near the cubbies, while the games and the language group worked at the semicircular table near the door. The books and puzzles area in the corner was used in the morning while waiting for all the children to arrive. The computer, books, and puzzles areas, and a play area for blocks, were used during choice time in the morning after centers.

Ms. Gomez's Resource Room Schedule

6 students, 2 staff

NAMES	T	R	A	D	J	To
8:30-8:45	Breakfast					
8:45-9:00	Journals and Table Tasks					
9:00-9:30	Morning Meeting					
9:30-9:50	Reading	IW	Reading	Math	Math	IW
9:50-10:10	IW	Math	IW	Reading	Reading	Math
10:10-10:30	Math	Reading	Math	IW	IW	Reading
10:30-10:45	Choice					
10:45-11:30	Lunch					
11:30-11:45	Grooming					
11:45-12:10	Playground					
12:10-12:30	Art	Art	Art	Games	Games	Games
12:30-12:50	Games	Games	Games	Art	Art	Art
12:50-1:30	Specials					
1:30-1:45	Snack					
1:45-2:00	Lang. Group	Social Grp.	Lang. Grp.	Social Grp.	Social Grp.	Lang. Grp.
2:00-2:15	Social Grp.	Lang. Grp.	Social Grp.	Lang. Grp.	Lang. Grp.	Social Grp.
2:15-2:30	Closing Group / Homenote					

IW = independent work.   Lang. Grp. = language group.

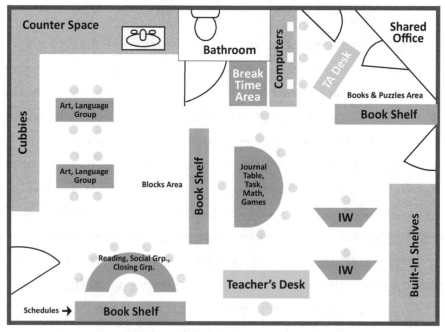

Ms. Gomez's "after" classroom layout.

This is an overall picture of the classroom. The photographer is standing by the door next to the morning meeting table. The teacher's desk is beyond that table, and the other group table is in the center of the room. Students can be seen working in the blocks area and in the books and puzzles area of the room. Visuals can be seen on the table indicating where the students should sit. This picture demonstrates how the areas are clearly defined and all areas can be supervised from any other area of the room.

The main group table accommodates morning meeting and afternoon group, reading center, and social group. The cutout feet on the floor in front of the door are in pairs for the students to line up with a buddy. The visuals on the board serve as calendar and sign-in for morning meeting; materials for all activities can be stored on the shelf by the board. Students' individual schedules are posted at the door. Some students in this room used a full day schedule, while others used the group schedule (next to the board) with a center strip only (next to the white visual schedule).

Small-group tables by cubbies accommodate art and language groups. The cubbies are for students to store their coats and other belongings. The space behind the shelf in the front of the picture serves as a blocks and manipulative play area.

Independent work area with work systems set up. The shelves on the left serve as storage for the tasks. As students' independence increases, they can begin to take the tasks off the shelf rather than the staff setting them up on the table before the students arrive. The TV is only used in the morning for the morning announcements, so it does not serve as a distracter. The students work left to right, placing the completed work in the "finished" basket to the right of their chair.

Summary

Designing the individual areas of the classroom takes careful consideration of the needs of all the students and the types of activities that will be taking place in the room. Making center rotations flow in a logical order, ensuring that a center's activity is not overly distracting to a center next to it, and arranging furniture in a way that prevents distractions are some of the strategies that create a successful learning environment for students with ASD.

ORGANIZING CLASSROOM MATERIALS

Having finished arranging her furniture, Ms. Wilson is getting ready to go out to dinner with a colleague, Ms. Harvey. Talking about her plans for her class, she describes the process she has gone through to arrange the furniture and talks about next steps. As she is talking, she suddenly realizes that she still has to put away her materials and make sure she has a variety of materials to support her students' learning.

"It is a lot of work up front, but in the end it makes the rest of the year so much easier. I just wish I didn't still have to figure out where to put my materials. It's not like I have a lot of materials, but I have to figure out how to store them so that my students don't get into them," she comments. Ms. Harvey offers, "I've worked with the principal for a number of years now, and I've found that he is really great about buying materials if you know what you need." Encouraged, Ms. Wilson starts to think about how to inventory the materials she has in her room and how she can arrange them to be easy to access and teach the students, and buy new ones if needed.

Faced with a different set of challenges, Ms. Gomez has been working with a classroom consultant, Dr. Diago, who has helped her arrange her furniture to meet the behavioral needs of her students. In working with Dr. Diago, it has become apparent that although Ms. Gomez has a lot of stuff in the room, much of it is incomplete or in disrepair. In addition, she does not always have the types of materials that her students need.

In response to Dr. Diago's observations, Ms. Gomez replied that she was waiting for the district to bring her new curriculum materials. Dr. Diago brought this up to the special education director, who said that Ms. Gomez had to inform her of what materials she needed. As part of the process of redesigning her room, Ms. Gomez has to clean out and inventory her materials and then make a list of curriculum materials that she needs to acquire to successfully set up appropriate instructional programs for her students.

As the scenarios of Ms. Wilson and Ms. Gomez illustrate, teachers must have the necessary materials to implement the classroom curriculum and each student's IEP. Knowing what types of materials will be needed is often an area of concern for teachers and administrators alike when setting up a classroom for students with ASD.

The following section provides information about acquiring and organizing appropriate materials for classrooms for students with ASD.

Classroom Supply Lists

The first step in designing any instructional program is to determine what materials are needed to teach various skills. For students with ASD who are included in the general education environment, many of the materials they will need are typically found in the general education classroom, except for any specialized materials and supports needed to make accommodations or modifications to the general education curriculum for them.

For students with more specialized learning needs who require an alternate curriculum, the types of materials they will need are often quite different from typical classroom materials. For instance, cardboard or plastic shoeboxes may be needed for holding tasks for independent work systems and organizing work for individual teaching sessions. Foam board or matte board may be needed to create large visuals and boards for communication and group participation activities. Common games and activities (e.g., scrapbooking, Yahtzee) may be needed to develop leisure and social skills. Specialized software, such as Boardmaker or Picture This (see Classroom Supply Lists), is often needed to make visual materials and icons for communication. These visuals, in turn, may have to be attached to notebooks and walls in the form of schedules and communication systems. (The most efficient manner to attach them is to use Velcro.) Many of the visuals shown in this book use Boardmaker icons (Mayer Johnson; www.mayer-johnson.com).

Further, visuals and materials must be laminated to protect them for everyday use by students in communication systems and learning activities such as file folder tasks. This makes heavy-duty laminate a highly sought-after item in most classrooms. Students, particularly those on the secondary level, typically are engaged in simulated work jobs and daily living activities. This requires purchasing materials for cooking, vocational activities, domestic tasks, and personal hygiene that usually are not part of a middle or high school classroom. In addition, due to their difficulty with motivation, specialized materials may be needed for fidget toys and concrete reinforcers, including food and common toys and trinkets (e.g., wind-up toys, tops).

The following lists help teachers request and acquire materials to equip their classrooms for successful learning. The lists offer options for preschool, elementary, and secondary learners. Understanding that most teachers do not have direct access to or control over the funds allocated for classroom materials, in some cases, the list offers alternatives of materials that are readily available.

Preschool and Elementary Basic Classroom Supply List

This list was developed based upon a classroom of 8 students with autism or related disabilities. It does not include basic office and classroom materials found in most general and special education classrooms. The materials are recommendations based on what we and teachers we have worked with have found to be useful and do not represent an endorsement of any certain product.

Item	Description/Examples	Quantity	Comments	Source
Assistive Technology and Computer Software Resources				
Voice output communication devices	Single switch, 2-cell, 4-cell, 8-cell, or others to meet individual needs	As needed		Mayer Johnson www.mayer-johnson.com/
Adapted keyboard and overlay maker	Intellikeys and Intellitools	1		IntelliTools www.intellitools.com
Picture symbol maker	*Boardmaker* and Addendum, *Picture This*	1		Mayer Johnson www.mayer-johnson.com/
	School Fonts CD			Mayer Johnson www.mayer-johnson.com
1 computer and color printer for making visuals and materials			May be in school computer lab	
Extra black and color print cartridges		2 each		
General Classroom Equipment				
CD/cassette player		2		
Language Master/card reader with cards		1		www.enasco.com
Headphones		4		
Digital timers		3		www.difflearn.com
Classroom Set-Up Materials				
White Velcro roll – bur strip – sticky back		50 yards		Lockfast www.lockfast.com
White Velcro roll – soft strip – sticky back		100 yards		www.lockfast.com
White Velcro roll – bur dots ¾ inch – sticky back		50 yards		www.lockfast.com
White Velcro roll – soft dots ¾ inch – sticky back		50 yards		www.lockfast.com
1" hard-sided binder loose-leaf notebooks for program books		1 per child		Office supply store
1" vinyl loose-leaf notebooks for PECS book		1 per child as needed		Office supply store
1 set of vinyl dividers for PECS book		1 per child as needed		Office supply store
Portable pouch laminator	USI	1	May use large school laminator, but usually it doesn't use laminate that is thick enough to be durable	USI www.usi-laminate.com

Item	Description/Examples	Quantity	Comments	Source
Letter- or legal-size pouch laminate: 5 ml and 7 ml	USI	150 sheets, 7 ml 100 sheets, 5 ml Opti-clear		USI www.usi-laminate.com
Regular dividers for each child's loose-leaf binder program book		1 set of 8 dividers per student		Office supply store
Vinyl (preferred) or other accordion jackets to use as check-in envelopes		8 envelopes		Office supply store
Clipboards		2 per student		Office supply store
Poster-sized sheets of foam board		6		Office supply store
Clear contact paper		1 large roll		Office supply store
Materials for Independent Work Systems				
Large rectangular laundry baskets for finished baskets		1 for each independent work station		Housewares
Clear plastic shoeboxes		At least 5 for each student	May also use cardboard boxes	Housewares
Plastic containers of various sizes to organize work task materials		10 square; 10 rectangle; 15 small round	May also use margarine containers	Housewares
Gallon-sized resealable plastic bags		50 bags		Housewares
Quart-sized resealable plastic bags		50 bags		Housewares
Wooden clothespins, spring loaded		2 packages		Housewares
Curriculum Materials				
Pattern blocks				Lakeshore Learning www.lakeshorelearning.com
1" cubes				www.lakeshorelearning.com
Counting bears		At least 100		www.lakeshorelearning.com
3-scene sequence cards		1		www.lakeshorelearning.com
4-scene sequence cards		1		www.lakeshorelearning.com
Math plastic links				www.lakeshorelearning.com
Musical instruments				www.lakeshorelearning.com
CDs for movement	*Let's Get Moving* CD Library			www.lakeshorelearning.com
Theme boxes	Farm, transportation, food, and nutrition			www.lakeshorelearning.com
Picture cards	*Language Builder* cards			Different Roads to Learning www.difflearn.com
Preschool and elementary activity books	File folder activity books			www.carsondellosa.com
	LinguiSystem *Concept Series*			www.linguisystems.com
	LinguiSystem *Functional Vocabulary for Children*			www.linguisystems.com
	Social Skills Stories			www.mayer-johnson.com
	More Social Skills Stories			www.mayer-johnson.com
	Math Exercises for Non-readers			www.mayer-johnson.com
	Noisy Stories			www.mayer-johnson.com
	Songs to Communicate			www.mayer-johnson.com
	Hands-on Reading			www.mayer-johnson.com
	More Hands-on Reading			www.mayer-johnson.com

Item	Description/Examples	Quantity	Comments	Source
Curricula	*Strategies for Teaching Based on Autism Research (STAR)*			Pro-Ed www.proedinc.com
	Skillstreaming for Early Childhood and *Skillstreaming the Elementary Child*			www.researchpress.com
	Teach Me Language			www.difflearn.com
	Do-Watch-Listen-Say			www.brookespublishing.com
	Edmark Level 1 and 2			www.proedinc.com
	Edmark Functional Word Series			www.proedinc.com
	Touch Math			www.touchmath.com
	Touch Math Time			www.touchmath.com
	Touch Math Money			www.touchmath.com
	Reading Milestones			www.proedinc.com
	Handwriting Without Tears			www.hwtears.com
	A Work in Progress			www.difflearn.com
	Teaching Language to Children with Autism or Other Developmental Disabilities *The Assessment of Basic Language and Learning Skills*			www.difflearn.com
Games and Leisure Materials				
	Lucky Ducks			Toy store
	Alphabet Bingo			www.lakeshorelearning.com
	Color and Shape Bingo			www.lakeshorelearnng.com
	Number Bingo			www.lakeshorelearning.com
	Dominoes			Toy store
	Listening Lotto			www.lakeshorelearning.com
	Uno			Toy store
	Candy Land			Toy store
Specialized Furniture				
	Educube	1 chair for each child as needed		Sensory Edge www.sensoryedge.com
	Edutrays for cube chairs	2-3 per room		www.sensoryedge.com

Secondary Basic Classroom Supply List

This list was developed based upon a classroom of 8 students with autism or related disabilities. It does not include basic office and classroom materials found in most general and special education classrooms. The materials are recommendations based on what we and teachers we have worked with have found to be useful and do not represent an endorsement of any certain product.

Item	Description/Examples	Quantity	Comments	
Assistive Technology and Computer Software Resources				
Voice-output communication devices	Single-switch, 2-cell, 4-cell, 8-cell, or others to meet individual needs	As needed		Mayer Johnson www.mayer-johnson.com
Adapted keyboard and overlay maker	Intellikeys and Intellitools	1		IntelliTools www.intellitools.com
Picture symbol maker	*Boardmaker* and Addendum, *Picture This*	1		Mayer Johnson www.mayer-johnson.com
	School Fonts CD			Mayer Johnson www.mayer-johnson.com
Computer and color printer for making visuals and materials			May be in school computer lab	
Extra black and color print cartridges		2 of each		
General Classroom Equipment				
CD/cassette player		2		
Language Master/card reader and cards		1		www.enasco.com
Headphones		4		
Digital timers		3		www.difflearn.com
Classroom Set-Up Materials				
White Velcro roll – bur strip, sticky back		50 yards		www.lockfast.com
White Velcro roll – soft strip, sticky back		100 yards		www.lockfast.com
White Velcro roll – bur dots ¾ inch, sticky back		50 yards		www.lockfast.com
White Velcro roll – soft dots ¾ inch, sticky back		50 yards		www.lockfast.com
1 " hard-sided binder loose-leaf notebooks for program books		1 per child		Office supply store
1" vinyl loose-leaf notebooks for PECS book		1 per student as needed		Office supply store
1 set of vinyl dividers for PECS book		1 per student as needed		Office supply store
Portable pouch laminator	USI	1	May use large school laminator, but it usually doesn't use laminate that is thick enough to be durable	USI www.usi-laminate.com

Item	Description/Examples	Quantity	Comments	
Letter- or legal-size pouch laminate: 5 ml and 7 ml	USI	7 ml: 150 sheets 5 ml: 100 sheets Opti clear		USI www.usi-laminate.com
Regular dividers for each student's loose-leaf binder program book		1 set of 8 dividers per student		Office supply store
Vinyl (preferred) or other accordion jackets to use as check-in envelopes		8 envelopes		Office supply store
Clipboards		2 per student		Office supply store
Poster-sized sheets of foam board		6		Office supply store
Clear contact paper		1 large roll		Office supply store
Materials for Independent Work Systems				
Large rectangular laundry baskets for finished baskets		1 for each independent work station		Housewares
Clear plastic shoeboxes		At least 5 for each student	Can also use cardboard boxes	Housewares
Plastic containers of various sizes to organize work task materials		10 square 10 rectangular 15 round	Can also use margarine containers	Supermarket
Gallon-sized resealable plastic bags		50 bags		Supermarket
Quart-sized resealable plastic bags		50 bags		Supermarket
Wooden clothespins, spring loaded		2 packages		Housewares
Wooden clothespins, peg type				Housewares
Washcloths		12		Housewares
Nuts and bolts		40 sets		Hardware
Silverware		1 set		Housewares
Red, blue, and black pens		2 packages of each		Office supply store
Pencils		2 packages		Office supply store
Pencil-top erasers		1 packages		Office supply store
Rice		2 bags		Supermarket
Measuring cups and spoons		2 sets		Housewares
Index card file boxes – assorted sizes		2		Office supply store
Dividers for file boxes – assorted sizes to match boxes		2 sets		Office supply store
Premade independent work tasks	Pre-Voc One by Attainment			Attainment Company www.attainmentcompany.com/
Curriculum Materials				
Picture vocabulary cards	Language Builder cards			Different Roads to Learning www.difflearn.com

Item	Description/Examples	Quantity	Comments	
Secondary activity books	*LIFE (Learning Independence through Functional Experiences)*			Mayer Johnson www.mayer-johnson.com
	Classroom to Workplace I and II			www.mayer-johnson.com
	Going Out and About			www.mayer-johnson.com
	RAPS (Reading Activities Project for Older Students)			www.mayer-johnson.com
	Stepping Out			www.attainmentcompany.com
	Cooking to Learn (2 vols.)			www.pcieducation.com
	Money math set			www.pcieducation.com
	Work Boxes			www.pcieducation.com
	Social Skills Stories			www.mayer-johnson.com
	Math Exercises for Nonreaders			www.mayer-johnson.com
	Menu Math			www.rempub.com
	Real-World Math			www.pcieducation.com
	Edmark Functional Word Series			www.proedinc.com
Curriculum	*Touch Money*			www.touchmath.com
	Touch Time			www.touchmath.com
	Murdoch Program Library			www.murdochfoundation.org
	Skillstreaming the Adolescent			www.researchpress.com
	Integrated Self-Advocacy ISA™ Model;			www.asperger.net
	The ECLIPSE Model			www.asperger.net
	Circles Curriculum			www.stanfield.com
	Functional Assessment & Curriculum for Teaching Everyday Routines (FACTER)			www.proedinc.com
	Functional Independence Skills Handbook – Assessment and Curriculum for Individuals with Developmental Disabilities (FISH)			www.proedinc.com
Games and Materials for Leisure Activities				
	Connect 4			Toy store
	Dominoes			Toy store
	Uno			Toy store
	Jenga			Toy store
	Craft materials			Craft store

Considerations When Choosing Materials

A number of factors must be considered when choosing materials for a classroom.

1. **Make sure that all materials are meaningful and motivating to the students.** This will increase the likelihood that they will attend to and participate in the instructional activities.

2. **Choose materials that are developmentally and age-appropriate while still being within the students' abilities and interests.** This is much easier when teaching young children than when working with older students with cognitive impairments. With older students, choose functional materials that can be used for skills that are at their developmental level. For instance, to teach counting to young children, counting bears or blocks may be used. When teaching the same skill to a student in high school, he or she could count coins or pens.

3. **Have a wide variety of materials available.** Students with ASD have difficulty generalizing skills to new materials, so it is important to have more than one set of materials with which to teach a skill.

4. **Be prepared. Have a sufficient quantity of materials to meet the needs of all students in the classroom during any given activity.** This prevents having to scavenge an area for materials while the student waits for instruction. For independent workers, this also prevents fighting over materials.

5. **Check periodically to make sure that all materials are in good repair.** This helps prevent the loss of time and frustration that typically occur if, in the middle of a lesson or activity, something is missing or broken and the activity either has to stop completely or students have to hunt for a replacement.

6. **Rotate materials frequently in order to continually challenge students.** Materials that are not being used should be stored so that they are not distracting to the current activities. Store nonessential materials in a closet, in a closed cabinet, or on a shelf with curtains or a similar covering to hide them from sight.

Considerations When Organizing Materials

An important component in ensuring that the classroom setup increases student engagement and decreases downtime involves organizing materials in such a way that time is not wasted looking for needed items throughout the day. When teachers have available in the activity area all the materials they need for a given activity, students can engage in the activity immediately upon transitioning. This means that students are more engaged, less time is wasted, and fewer challenging behaviors occur.

The following recommendations help ensure that materials are available and in good repair to be accessed with as little effort as possible by staff and/or students.

1. **Store materials in the area where they are most likely to be used.** For example, place art materials in the area where art takes place. Similarly, during 1:1 and small-group preacademic or academic instruction, organize and store the materials needed to support instruction for each child in the area. That allows access to materials needed for instruction without the teacher having to leave the students she is working with, which in turn could lead to students becoming off task or engaging in challenging behavior.

2. **Organize materials to support the skills targeted for students.** If a student is working on requesting, for example, put materials out of reach of the student so he will have to ask/request desired/needed items. Similarly, if students are learning to share, avoid having enough materials for each child to have his own, forcing children to share and take turns. If students are working on independence, make materials accessible to the students.

3. **Organize and make accessible materials that support instruction**. Store the visual supports that are used to accompany activities in the area where they are used. Keep clipboards with data sheets near the activities to which they relate. A variety of storage containers are available to make this easy, such as rolling carts, plastic shoeboxes, zipper plastic bags, stacking trays, and file folders.

4. **Be consistent with the use of Velcro within the school.** We prefer to use the bur (hook) Velcro on the movable pieces while putting the softer, loop, Velcro on the surfaces. We refer to this rule as "hard on the card, soft on the surface." This system allows the user to Velcro icons on things like dividers that are covered in material. While decisions about how to place the Velcro is left up to the user, it is critical that the classroom, family, or school use the same system throughout to avoid having visuals that cannot be used in other situations because the Velcro is not compatible.

Instructional materials are organized by student; clipboards holding data sheets for each of the three groups are kept in the area.

Instructional materials are organized by student or by subject.

Each child's data sheets attached to a clipboard are stored in a basket. The basket is transported to the instructional area by a student as a helper job during the first transition to centers.

Independent work tasks are stored in a set of shelves; they may be organized by student or by type of task.

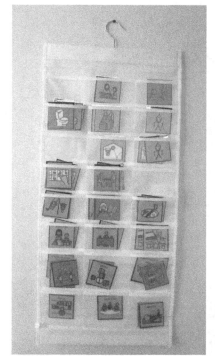

(Left) Visuals for the schedule are stored in a pocket shoe organizer.

(Below) Schedule visuals are stored in individual small plastic containers and placed in a basket.

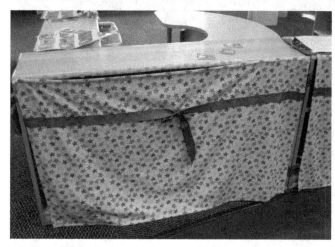

Decorative curtains can hide the materials in shelving units if they cause a distraction for students. (Notice how the curtains are nicely finished. They are attached by Velcro.)

Summary

Having materials well organized, labeled, and accessible where needed ensures that more time can be spent instructing students in a planful manner. A good way to ensure that materials will be where and when they are needed is to keep a running list in the room and write down every time something is not located in an area where it is needed. Then, at the end of the day, check the list and move the materials to the proper location if needed. Taking the time to plan and organize materials, as well as periodically reviewing and clearing out old materials – and replenishing as necessary – will increase the enjoyment and long-range benefits of both teaching and learning in the classroom.

USING VISUAL CUES TO ORGANIZE CLASSROOMS FOR EFFECTIVE LEARNING

Ms. Wilson presented her list of materials to her principal and was very pleased to find that he agreed to buy everything she requested. One of the things she needed desperately was a way to make visuals. She knew that she needed schedules and communication systems, but first she had to make visuals to complete her organization of the classroom.

Ms. Wilson's classroom was coming together. She had a schedule established and had the furniture she needed to make her schedule work. She had her furniture arranged and her materials organized when her colleague, Ms. Harvey, came back to visit the classroom. Ms. Harvey started to help Ms. Wilson clean up the materials. However, when she started to do so, she was not sure where the materials went. Her questions for direction gave Ms. Wilson the idea that she needed to put pictures on the shelves so that both the staff and the students would know where to put materials when cleaning up after an activity.

Ms. Gomez's students were behaving much more positively since the change in the room design and the acquisition of more motivating materials that were in good repair. The students were no longer running around the room, climbing on the furniture, or leaving their instructional areas. However, there were still a few times during the day that were difficult for them, causing them to exhibit some of their old challenging behaviors. One of those times was lining up to go outside.

To address this issue, Dr. Diago suggested that Ms. Gomez put visuals on the floor, like feet, to show the students where to stand to line up. Ms. Gomez thought this was kind of silly. Nevertheless, the next day, she taped footprints to the floor in the form of a line and told the students to "stand on the feet." To her amazement, all the students lined up on the markers, without touching each other or misbehaving the way they usually did. In fact, this worked so well that she decided to use other types of visual cues throughout the room to help students know where to sit, stand, and wait during the day.

In the following, we will look at various kinds of visual cues and their roles in effective classrooms. As illustrated in the cases of Ms. Wilson and Ms. Gomez, visual cues help both students and staff.

Visual Cues for Students

Everybody uses a variety of visual cues every day in all environments. For example, when standing in line at the Department of Motor Vehicles to get a driver's license, people face a sign that says, "Wait here for the next available clerk." This is a visual that tells us where to wait. When crossing the street, we use Walk/Don't Walk signs that tell us when it is safe to walk or when we should stop. These signs (i.e., visuals) tell us how to behave.

Students with ASD generally have better developed visual skills than auditory skills. Therefore, visual supports are an effective way to teach skills and build independence within the classroom environment for these students. Visuals may be used in a variety of ways to support the arrangement of the physical environment, including showing students ...

- where to sit
- where to stand
- where to line up
- where to go next
- what to attend to
- where to put things
- which activities and choices are available

Visuals to indicate where to sit. Place pictures or nametags on a chair, table, or floor to indicate where a specific student is supposed to sit. In addition to directing students where to sit, this also helps teachers control where students sit (e.g., it makes it easy to separate students who do not work well when sitting next to each other; conversely, it makes it easy to seat students who are working on sharing or interacting near each other). Within a general education classroom, such visuals can subtly serve to save a special place for the student with ASD near the teacher to increase attention, or on the outskirts of a group to reduce sensory overload.

Tape on the floor may indicate the area where a student is expected to remain for an activity. For instance, a student who constantly moves his chair toward the teacher in a group activity may be better able to stay in his place if tape is put down on the floor in a box around his chair.

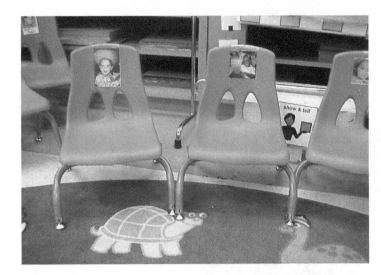

This teacher uses pictures on the back of the children's chairs to give cues about where to sit at circle time.

A cutout may be taped to the floor and labeled with the child's name so he knows where to sit during morning meeting.

This table is labeled with each child's name so the children know where they are to sit and where their work area is.

Each child's name is taped to the table so both staff and child know where students are to sit. This also allows separating students who do not interact well to prevent problem behaviors.

Masking tape is used on the floor of a first-grade general education classroom to mark where students are to sit.

Visuals to indicate where to stand. Markers may be placed on the floor to let students know where to stand and wait for an activity. This can help to ensure that a student does not hover over another student while waiting her turn; it may also help reduce anxiety for the student with ASD by assuring him that he is next in line. Common areas in classrooms for this type of visuals include the sink for washing hands, outside the computer area, and near the teacher's desk.

The tape on the floor with the blue and red marks (bottom of the photo) indicates where students are to stand to wait to use the sensory equipment.

Visuals to indicate where to line up. Cutouts of feet or other types of markers may be taped to the floor by the door to tell students where to stand to line up to leave the room. Markers may be placed with enough distance between them to ensure that students cannot touch each other. Markers may be placed in one line for single-file lines or in double lines for walking with a buddy. Names may be added by the markers to make it clear where specific students are to stand in the lineup. This is particularly helpful to separate students who have a history of demonstrating inappropriate behaviors when near each other.

Cutout feet are taped to the floor where children line up so that they maintain appropriate space between each other. The child's name is on the line between the two feet.

Here is another example of feet on the floor leading to the door through which the children exit the room.

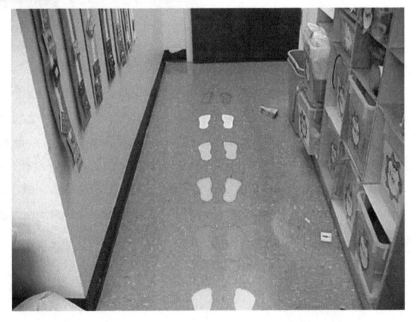

Here the cutout feet are placed between two sheets of contact paper because the teacher cannot tape feet to the floor. Velcro on the bottom of the contact paper allows it to grip the carpet. The set of feet may be moved to other parts of the school as needed to assist students in lining up appropriately.

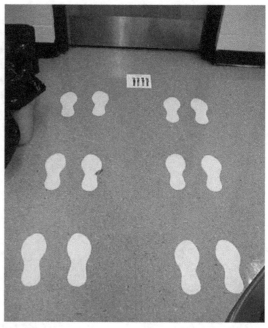

If children are working on social skills, the feet may be placed in pairs so that children walk with a partner.

Visuals to indicate where to go next. In addition to other uses, students with ASD benefit from the use of visual schedules to increase independence in following the classroom routine. For students who are using a schedule that requires manipulating a card with an icon, object, or word, each activity should have a check-in area or "landing" pad. Landing pads can be envelopes, boards with Velcro, or containers with a picture, word, or object that matches the schedule piece. Students take their card from their schedules and check in at the activity with the corresponding visual. Individuals with ASD have difficulty with transitions and often spend significant amounts of time worried about what will come next. Schedules help these students to focus on the work at hand and to understand, not worry about, what comes next.

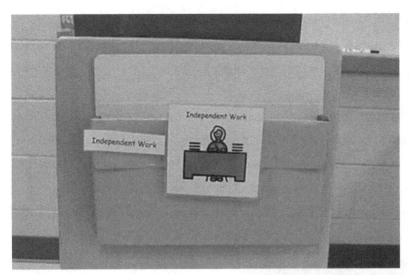

Check-in envelopes may be attached to furniture with Velcro. These are accordion folders with the forward flap folded down and stapled and the picture and word for students to match. These envelopes also come in vinyl in packages of four (see Classroom Supply Lists).

Both object and picture are attached to the check-in envelope. Make sure to have the same type of schedule pieces on the check-in envelope as your students use.

Visuals to indicate what to attend to. Many students with ASD are easily distracted by visual stimuli in their environment. To prevent them from becoming overstimulated or distracted, it is important that the visual materials used in the room are useful and functional for the chosen activities.

Generally, if the class has visual schedules, communication tools such as Picture Exchange Communication System (PECS) books, and students' work displayed in the room, there is little need to add more, often superfluous, decorations. The following recommendations regarding placement and use of visual material help ensure that visual cues are useful, functional, and accessible to all the students in the room.

1. **When presenting students' work and visuals, whether artwork, papers, or schedules, display them at the students' eye level so that they can appreciate it and use it.** Bulletin boards in the hallway may be used for these purposes as well, particularly if there is a student in the room who rips materials off the walls.

2. **Evaluate for each student the classroom practice of putting projects on paper clips hanging from ceiling tiles to see if this practice will be effective for the class.** That is, some students are distracted by materials hanging from the ceiling, while others are not bothered by this practice.

3. **Make sure students are easily able to reach their visual tools and communication systems throughout the day.** If working with young children, teachers should consider walking through the classroom on their knees to see what items they can and cannot access easily and safely. Many times schedules, in an attempt to fit the full day's activities on the wall, start higher than the student can easily reach, making them less functional for the student.

4. **In addition to reviewing and removing irrelevant items that may distract students, highlight work areas on assignments and within activities to help students to more independently achieve specific tasks.** For an included student, this may mean highlighting relevant vocabulary on a worksheet assigned to the whole class. For another student, it may mean using sticker dots on a vending machine to highlight the important steps in buying a soda (e.g., one by the coin slot, one by the button for the desired soda, and one by the change outlet).

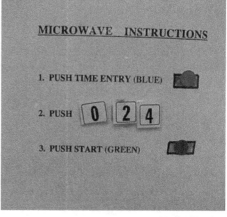

Color-coded dots are placed on the microwave to go with the visual directions.

Color-coded dots are placed on the vending machine to tell the student which areas of the machine he or she needs to use.

Labeling Shelves and Cabinets

Labeling shelves and cabinets with pictures and/or words serves three functions:

1. It helps both students and staff to know where materials are stored for easy access.

2. It helps students and staff to know where to return materials after use.

3. It pairs the printed word with objects for literacy.

The cabinets are labeled with the word and the picture for the items that are stored. This is important in this secondary classroom where the students are expected to put away the dishes after washing them.

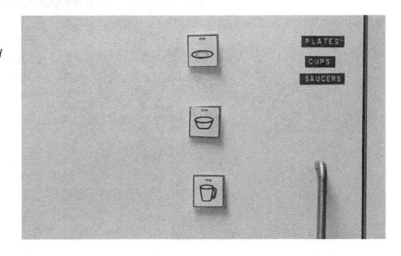

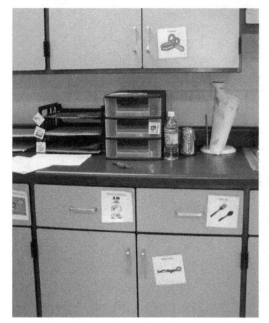

(Left) These cabinets are labeled with Boardmaker visuals to show the contents and where to return items.

(Below) This is a set of cabinets in a kitchen in a group home, where all drawers and cabinets are labeled with the pictures for what goes in each area. The photos on top show the steps in a recipe.

Each child's cubby area is marked with his or her name.

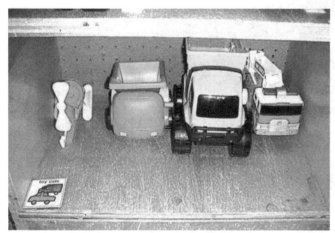

Shelves in the play area are marked with the picture of what is stored in the area. This makes it easy for both students and staff to clean up.

A job task for older students is stored in a container with the directions written on it. The directions are in text format for students who are able to read or to help buddies support the student with the task.

Plastic containers are labeled with the names of the materials that are stored within. Photos of the items are also taped to the containers.

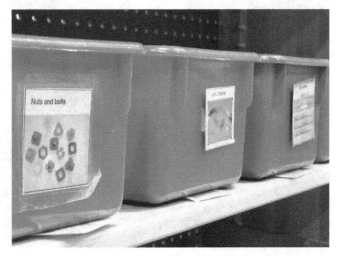

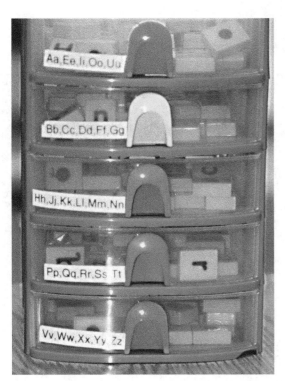

Letter tiles are stored in the drawers labeled with the letters that are contained in each.

Visuals to Mark Available Versus Off-Limits Activities

A variety of visual cues may be used to inform students of whether something is available or not. For example, computers, a frequent distraction for students with ASD, may be covered with a sheet or a box, a stop sign, or a sign that says "finished" to indicate when they are not available for use. Choice boards that allow students to see when a center or activity is open, full, or closed for the day can help them make decisions and anticipate options. Making the options visually clear can help reduce students' anxiety and prevent challenging behaviors due to disappointment and violated expectations. Areas of the room can be blocked with a sign that says, "Stop" to indicate that it is off limits.

This center check-in board tells students that the art area is closed. Each child has a colored clothespin and marks the center he will work in.

The sign on the computer monitor tells the students that the computer is not available at this time.

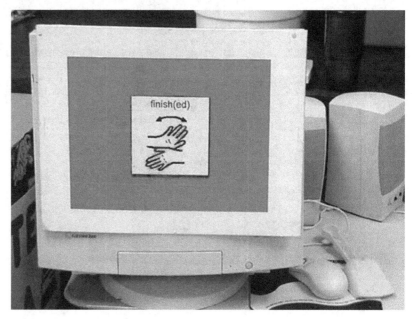

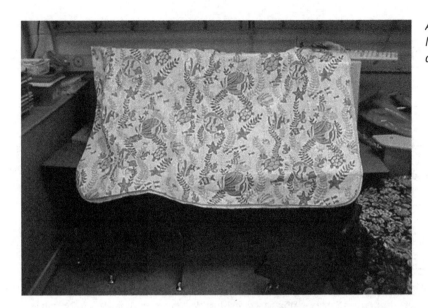

A quilt is draped over the computers to let the students know that the computer area is closed.

We all make use of visual strategies every day, often totally unconsciously. We go to the supermarket and stand in the checkout lines where the numbers are lit up. We stop before crossing the street when the light is red ... the list goes on and on.

Similarly, visual cues help students with ASD to make sense of their environment. By being able to rely on predictable cues in the classroom, they are more comfortable and, therefore, in a better position to focus more time on instruction. That is, the energy otherwise spent on worrying about what will come next can now be constructively expended on learning.

To be successful, visual cues must be clear and readily available. In addition, students must learn to understand and use each type of cue before they can rely on it on a regular basis.

A good rule of thumb is to have a colleague come into the classroom and look at the materials displayed. Can he or she identify the function of each of the materials? If so, then the materials are probably relevant and needed. If the function is difficult to discern or if the visual is not related to the running of the classroom (e.g., a bulletin board decorated with fall leaves when none of the lesson plans address seasons or leaves), consider removing that item and storing the material elsewhere.

Designing effective classroom environments for students with ASD is more complicated than simply putting out desks and chairs. The unique characteristics of ASD and their impact on students' learning styles and ability to navigate complex environments make careful consideration and planning of their instructional environments a key component of effective intervention.

The following is a synopsis of warning signs and solutions to potential difficulties observed in classrooms that can be addressed by changes in the physical environment. These warning signs are provided as an overview to help teachers think about issues in their own classrooms and how the physical environment may impact them.

Warning Signs of Problems With the Physical Environment and Possible Solutions

Warning Sign: If your students are ...	Solution: You should ...
Running in the classroom	Use furniture to structure empty space or "runways," such as around tables
Climbing on furniture	Move the furniture to a location that's more difficult to access, such as against a wall
Wandering the room without being engaged	Review visual cues that give direction about where student should be
Distracted by other activities in the room	Move the distracting areas away from quiet areas requiring more concentration
Touching or fighting with each other in line	Put markers on the floor indicating where to stand
Moving their chairs at the table or on the floor to bother another student	Put markers on the floor or the table rather than the chair
Touching others' materials at the table	Use masking or electrical tape to make a boundary of each child's space at the table. Use placemats with the children's names as a place to put their materials and teach them to only touch things on their own mat. Put the students' materials on a cookie sheet on the table – choose one with edges to give clear boundaries
Not cleaning up their materials at the end of the activity	Use visual cues to indicate where the materials should go
Repeating activities over and over without completing them	Indicate a clear place to put material when it is finished (e.g., finished bin or basket)
Constantly asking to go to a desired activity that is not available	Put an X marker, stop sign, or finished sign on the entry to the activity or material to indicate when it's time to use it; put a clock with the time it is available on the item
Leaving the area of an activity	Use shelves to mark boundaries to indicate where they should remain
Leaving the table during small group or 1:1 instruction	Turn the table so that the student's back is against the wall and the table is between the instructor and student
Frequently distracted by the other activities in the room while in a small-group instructional activity	Turn the table so the students are facing the wall for fewer distractions
Keeping materials in the area	Use walls and furniture to create clear areas, and label cabinets and shelves with pictures or words of what belongs there
Spending too much time looking for specific materials during instructional time	Organize materials for instruction in bins or bags by student or by skill to be taught (e.g., all the sequencing cards together) and store in a cart or cabinet for easy access
Wandering away before an activity begins	Make sure that materials are set up for the activity before the students arrive at the area so they can be immediately engaged
Looking out the window instead of at the teacher	Move the furniture so the student faces the teacher directly
Looking at other things in the room rather than the work or the teacher	Review the visual materials in the room to ensure that they are functionally related to the instruction and eliminate decorative materials that are not related to or products of activities
Engaging in inappropriate behaviors that are related to difficulty communicating	Ensure that communication supports and systems are readily available to the students in every area of the classroom so students will not have to leave the area to obtain them
Dumping materials off shelves or tables regularly	Cover the shelves with curtains or sheets to put materials not being used out of sight. Make sure that tables only display the materials needed for a given activity. Keep materials needed for the tables in closed bins next to the teacher's chair at the activity to prevent early access by the students

Summary

Teachers of students with ASD have different needs for furniture and materials than general education teachers and even most other teachers in special education. We hope the resources and ideas in this book for organizing classroom environments will help teachers successfully engage students in instruction and social interactions and, ultimately, ensure better learning outcomes and independent, self-confident students.

FREQUENTLY ASKED QUESTIONS

The following are questions raised by professionals we have met during our years of working in a variety of settings for students with ASD. The questions address some of the most common concerns we have encountered and are presented here in an attempt to provide some ideas for solving difficult situations when addressing classroom design.

Q: What if you don't have an extensive budget to buy materials for your classroom?

A: Several strategies can be used to make or acquire materials for your classroom. Magazine pictures and images from the Internet may be used to make picture cards and file folder matching tasks. Pictures from magazines or digital photos can be used to make schedules. We have listed several Internet resources in the resource section of this book that provide these types of visuals, if you do not have software to create them.

A wide variety of materials can also be made with common household objects such as clothespins, index cards, file folders, and popsicle sticks. For instance, a matching-word-to-picture task may be constructed by writing the word on clothespins and putting a picture from a magazine on an index card and having the students clip the clothespin to the appropriate index card.

Also, if you do not have laminate readily available or if the laminate at your school is too thin, mount pictures on cardstock or file folders, cut them out, and use clear contact paper or heavy-duty clear packing tape to provide a protective covering.

If students are likely to destroy materials or if materials wear out quickly, consider going to a local framing shop and asking if the owner is willing to donate scraps of matte board for you to mount the visuals on before covering them. Visuals we have made this way have lasted for years. Matte board also serves as a good material to make choice boards and other display materials for group activities within the classroom.

Q: Are Boardmaker icons better than photographs when structuring a classroom?

A: There are many ways to make schedules and other visual cues within the classroom. Boardmaker is a software program that allows users to make symbolic pictures of activities and items that can then be consistent across classrooms and environments. This allows students to use their schedule in other environments and understand that the meaning of the icon indicates the activity rather than the physical place.

However, some students have difficulty understanding the iconic pictures and do better with photographs. Yet other students with ASD focus on inconsequential items in photographs and fail to equate them with the setting if a given element is missing (e.g., the student sees markers on the table in the photo for the art area, but sees paints on the art table in her classroom and fails to understand they are the same table). Some students need an object schedule using three-dimensional items that represent different activities in the room rather than images. For instance, a spoon may represent lunch or computer keys may represent the media center.

Like many decisions regarding students with ASD, teachers must take into consideration students' individual needs. We generally start with Boardmaker pictures and make modifications if the student does not begin to learn how to use the schedule successfully.

Q: I am using visual supports and clear boundaries in my self-contained classroom, but my student is having trouble in his general education classroom. What can I do?

A: If a student is using a certain strategy successfully in a more specialized environment, it is critical that similar strategies be adapted and used in inclusive environments. For example, students who require instruction in secluded environments, free of distractions of large classrooms, typically require more support in larger, more inclusive environments. However, we often forget this and send students off to specials or other activities with the general education students without providing the visual and physical support that is essential to their success.

All environments require some level of adaptation to make strategies within them successful for students with ASD. For instance, if a student is using a visual schedule on the wall in the resource room, he could take a folder or notebook with the visuals needed for the time he spends in the general education classroom and keep that on his desk to use. If a student needs a structured work system with a clear finished spot to work independently in the resource room, she could have a Trapper Keeper type of folder with her work in it and a finished folder at the back of the system that she uses in the general education classroom. Or, if she needs a more formal, structured system, there could be a structured place in the general education classroom where she could complete her work independently with a "finished" basket while the other students are doing independent activities.

Q: Will my students need visual cues forever?

A: The goal of using visual cues is to help students become more independent and less in need of teacher and staff directions and support. If a student is able to complete an activity with a visual schedule or visual task analysis without the teacher standing beside her, she is more independent.

One of the ultimate goals would be to reduce the use of visual cues by fading them from the environment to build even more student independence. Ways to do this includes making the visuals smaller, making them lighter (using a photocopy machine), or gradually leaving off individual visuals from the end of the schedule, one at a time, so that eventually the student is using only the first visual as a cue. Similarly, when using visual cues within the physical structure of the room (e.g., using masking tape to outline a place to sit), pieces of the barrier could be removed systematically to gradually make the line on the floor or the marker less noticeable until it eventually disappears.

In each of these scenarios, the teacher is fading the visual support. It is important, however, to make sure that visuals are not faded too quickly and to understand that while students may not need the visual support in one setting (e.g., resource room), they may still need it in others (e.g., general education classroom).

All of us use visual cues during our daily activities. We make notes to ourselves, keep a calendar or planner for our daily schedule, and have lists of work we expect to accomplish within a certain time period. These are all forms of visual supports, and none of us expects to fade out the use of planners, for example. The same goes for the visuals used by students with ASD: Some of them they may need to use them forever to be able to function smoothly and successfully.

A goal for students would be to try to make their visual supports more and more like those used in the general environment in which they interact. Transferring a visual schedule to a day planner that might be used in middle school is a good example. However, remember not to fade the visuals too quickly and be aware if the student starts to require more adult attention and support in the form of direction and redirection. This is often a sign that the student continues to need the visual support to be independent of teacher and staff assistance.

Q: One of my students grabs other students' schedules. How can I prevent this from happening?

A: Generally, all students' schedules are posted in the same area in the classroom. This can have the unintended effect of (a) confusing some students about which schedule belongs to which student and (b) allowing students for whom the schedule is less meaningful or more difficult to understand to get in the way of students who are faster and more independent in using them. It can also allow students to take another student's schedule pieces.

One way to address all of these issues is as simple as distributing the schedules across different parts of the room, rather than placing them all in one area on the wall. We once worked in a classroom that had large support columns in the middle of the room. While it was difficult to arrange activities around them, the columns served as excellent places to post individual schedules. We were able to put one schedule on each side of the square pillars, needing 3 pillars for our 12 students. In this way, four schedules were located in the same place without being right next to each other, helping to limit the number of hands that would touch the schedule to the one student who actually needed to use it.

Q: I have a structured classroom, but my students don't use it correctly. What do I do?

A: Unfortunately, putting the structure into the classroom is only the first part of the process. Students will not necessarily know how to use the strategies described in this book on their own – the systems must be taught. For example, students must be taught to stay in a certain area and that the shelf is a boundary for how far they can move within the area. The best way to teach this skill is to have highly engaging materials for students to interact with and reinforce them with desired activities, items, and praise for remaining in the area.

Similarly, visual schedules and visual markers must be taught before students understand how to use them. Students should be reinforced for sitting in the correct spot on the floor or at the table and for using their schedule appropriately. Becoming familiar with the routine of the classroom and how to use the systems are often some of the first goals for students when they enter school. Students who have not used these systems before need time to get used to and learn them. This, in turn, will allow them to stop thinking about the structure and start focusing on the work within the structure – the ultimate goal behind all of this.

Q: How do I teach my student to stay inside boundaries that I have identified in the classroom?

A: One of the prerequisites for helping students to stay within an area of the classroom is to make sure that they are engaged from the moment they walk into the area and that activities involve materials that are interesting and engaging to them ... and that they can easily access. If this condition has been met and the student still wanders or runs from the area, the student must be taught directly to stay in the area.

One of the best ways to teach something is to reinforce the student for doing it. This means identifying highly preferred items and activities and providing them to the student when he is within the designated area. If you don't know what your student likes or what would be reinforcing for him, put out a variety of materials and see what he chooses to play or interact with. When you find something that is interesting to him, look for other items that have some of the same characteristics. For instance, we worked with a student once who, when left to wander the full classroom, got a piece of tape, turned it inside out (with the sticky side on the outside), and began to play with it with his fingers touching the sticky material.

Clearly, tape is not a material used in all types of instruction, nor was it an age-appropriate toy for this preschooler. To find suitable alternatives (i.e., items with the same characteristics), we went to a toy store and found all sorts of sticky toys that could serve as reinforcers. By using the sticky toys as a reinforcer for following our directions, we had the student sitting in his chair and adhering to simple directions very quickly. As long as access to the sticky toys was conditional to his remaining in the area, he didn't leave the area during instruction.

Q: My student's parents report that at home he climbs on the furniture, doesn't sit at the table to eat, and won't pick up his toys. How can I help his parents to structure their home environment?

A: Students are likely to have similar problems at home and at school. Yet, many parents report that their child has more difficulty at home than at school. This is in part because of the highly structured nature of school routines and environments, which are difficult to replicate within the context of family life.

One way to help parents is to assist them in identifying short periods of the day that are most difficult (e.g., while making dinner in the evening, around bedtime, just after coming home from school) and help to establish a routine for just that part of the day, rather than expecting a parent to schedule the whole day for the child. Then volunteer to make visuals to depict the routine for bedtime or the routine for coming home from school to help the student understand the expectations.

Specific activities can also be set up for specific areas. For instance, the child could do a series of art projects at the kitchen table while the parents are making dinner. An independent work system could be set up with coloring pages and other art projects that the student can complete independently, followed by a schedule that indicates that the use of the computer is allowed after the list of work is finished. This provides an incentive for the child to complete the activities while reducing computer time during dinner preparation.

Providing visuals and other supports to families and helping them to set up routines within manageable time frames can help to reduce the amount of support their children need to complete their chores, do their homework, and get ready for activities. Your assistance will probably be needed to help parents break down the routine activities in addition to providing the visuals. A home visit may help accomplish this. It is time well spent!

Q: A paraprofessional supports my student in a general education classroom and tends to hover over the student or sit right beside her. How can I help the paraprofessional make the student more independent?

A: Often paraprofessionals serve as primary supports for students with ASD in the general education classroom. It is critical that the paraprofessional knows what is expected of her within that role. This includes understanding that the student must learn to be as independent as possible when outside the special education classroom.

First, paraprofessionals must know the student's IEP goals and objectives. Paras are being expected to assist in teaching a student; without knowing what the student is expected to learn and do, this task is impossible to do well.

Second, the team must decide what the goals are for each activity in which the student is participating throughout the day. This includes the activities in which he engages in the general education classroom. Specific goals for these times of the day are critical to the student being successful in these environments. For instance, is the student expected to work at grade level and do the same work as the other students? If so, what accommodations should be planned in advance for the paraprofessional to provide? Is the student being included to enhance social opportunities and skills? If so, how is this to be done within the activity? If a student is included to enhance social opportunities, it is critical to make sure that those social opportunities exist within the time the student spends in the classroom.

Take the example of a student who is included for middle school science. Is the student expected to complete the science lab at grade level as the other students in the class? If so, the paraprofessional must know the lesson that is planned and how it can be accommodated, if needed, for the student. Is the student participating in order to learn the science material, but not at the same grade level or with the same presentation of the material as the other students? If so, what modifications can the paraprofessional make in the way the material is presented, or is there an alternate assignment that the paraprofessional should give to the student to complete? Is the student expected to participate for socialization opportunities rather than the science curriculum material? If so, can the science experiment be pretaught in the special education classroom so that the paraprofessional can pair the student with a student or students from the general education classroom to complete the lab with a focus on asking for materials, talking to the other student(s), and participating in the activity itself independent of the paraprofessional? Without knowing what the expectations are for the student, the para cannot be expected to provide the needed support and fade out as appropriate.

Another common problem with personnel support in the general education classroom is deciding where the paraprofessional should be positioned. In many classrooms, it is assumed that the paraprofessional is there to support all or multiple students and that he or she moves around the room much as the teacher does. However, in some cases, the student with ASD needs more specific and individualized support than this scenario would allow.

One way to help the paraprofessional to move in and provide support when needed but still fade out when the student functions more independently is to have a rolling stool or chair available that the para can use to move toward the student and away without having to remain on his or her feet throughout the class.

Another critical element in building independence is for the para to have a book or container of common visuals that the student may need. Visuals for communication, schedules, redirection, and work systems should all be stored in an easy-to-access system (e.g., notebook) that the para can access and use as needed from a distance. This will reduce the number of verbal redirections that the para must provide to help the student be successful and help to fade assistance as the student becomes more independent.

Q: My student, who is nonverbal, often leaves the instructional area to get his communication device. What do I do?

A: If you have a student who uses a device or other supports for communication, the device must be available to him throughout the day. If the student is able to learn to carry the device with a strap during his day, he should be taught to be responsible for moving it with him from area to area. If the device is too heavy or bulky, or if the student struggles with carrying it or being responsible for it, the device may be stored in a common area in the classroom (and in a bin in a common area in each environment outside the classroom).

Further, to prevent the student from being redirected each time he attempts to get up to access the device because the teacher thinks he is leaving the area, a card that says "I need to get my device" may be placed in each area and be readily available to the student to give to the teacher to indicate that he is getting his communication device. This may help to make clear his intent in leaving and make using his device as efficient as possible.

APPENDIX

Instructional Resources – Books

The following lists consists of books that we have found useful in helping teachers plan and implement instruction in their classrooms and providing background information on appropriate strategies for students with ASD. This list does not represent an endorsement of any the books.

Aspy, R., & Grossman, B. J. (2007). *The Ziggurat model: A framework for designing comprehensive interventions with individuals with high-functioning autism and Asperger syndrome.* Shawnee Mission, KS: Autism Asperger Publishing Company. **Elementary, Secondary**

The Blackwell Family. (2009). *2010 hidden curriculum one-a-day calendar for kids: Items for understanding unstated rules in social situations* (calendar). Shawnee Mission, KS: Autism Asperger Publishing Company. **Elementary**

Buron, K. D. (2010-2011). *The social times.* (Monthly magazine for students grades 3-10) Shawnee Mission, KS: Autism Asperger Publishing Company. **Elementary, Secondary**

Coyne, P., Nyberg, C., & Vandenburg, M. L. (1999). *Developing leisure time skills for persons with autism: A practical approach for home, school, and community.* Arlington, TX: Future Horizons. **Elementary, Secondary**

Endow, J. (2009). *2010 hidden curriculum one-a-day calendar for older adolescents and adults: Items for understanding unstated rules in social situations* (calendar). Shawnee Mission, KS: Autism Asperger Publishing Company. **Secondary**

Endow, J. (2009). *Outsmarting explosive behavior: A visual system of support and intervention for individuals with autism spectrum disorders.* Shawnee Mission, KS: Autism Asperger Publishing Company. **Elementary, Secondary**

Freeman, S. K., & Dake, D. (1997). *Teach me language: A language manual for children with autism, Asperger 's syndrome, and related developmental disorders.* Langley, BC, Canada: SKF Books. **Preschool, Elementary, Secondary**

Frost, L., & Bondy, A. (2002). *The picture exchange communication system training manual* (2nd ed.). Newark, DE: Pyramid Educational Products, Inc. **Preschool, Elementary, Secondary**

Grandin, T., & Duffy, K. (2008). *Developing talents: Careers for individuals with Asperger syndrome and high functioning autism* (updated, expanded edition). Shawnee Mission, KS: Autism Asperger Publishing Company. **Elementary, Secondary**

Henry, S., & Myles, B. S. (2007). *The comprehensive autism planning system (CAPS) for individuals with Asperger syndrome, autism, and related disabilities: Integrating best practices throughout the student's day.* Shawnee Mission, KS: Autism Asperger Publishing Company. **Preschool, Elementary, Secondary**

Hodgdon, L. (1995). *Visual strategies for improving communication: Practical supports for school and home.* Troy, MI: Quirk Roberts Publishing. **Preschool, Elementary, Secondary**

Myles, B. S., & Adreon, D. (2001). *Asperger syndrome and adolescence: Practical solutions for student success.* Shawnee Mission, KS: Autism Asperger Publishing Company. **Secondary**

Packer, A. J. (1997). *How rude!: The teenager's guide to good manners, proper behavior, and not grossing people out.* Minneapolis, MN: Free Spirit Publishing. **Secondary**

Resources for Arranging the Physical Environment

The following are resources directly related to the design of classrooms and the materials within them. This is not intended to be an exhaustive list, nor is it intended to indicate endorsement of any of the items in the list. It simply includes resources that we have found to be useful in gaining ideas for classroom setups.

Video

Dodge, D. T., & Kittredge, B. (2003). *Room arrangement as a teaching strategy.* Washington, DC: Teaching Strategies.

Books

Beston, S. M. (1999). *How to organize your classroom*. Westminster, CA: Teacher Created Materials, Inc.

Chang, M. L. (2004). *Classroom management in photographs: Full-color photographs with teacher descriptions and insights about what really works*. New York: Scholastic.

Clayton, M. K., & Forton, M. B. (2001). *Classroom spaces that work*. Greenfield, MA: Northeast Foundation for Children.

Isbell, R., & Exelby, B. (2001). *Early learning environments that work*. Beltsville, MD: Gryphon House.

Loughlin, C. E. & Suina, J. H. (1982). *The learning environment: An instructional strategy*. New York: Teachers College Press.

Articles

Hauser-Cram, P., Bronson, M. B., & Upshur, C. C. (1993). The effects of the classroom environment on the social and mastery behavior of preschool children with disabilities. *Early Childhood Research Quarterly, 8*(4), 479-497.

Schmidt, L. (1995). *Child care by design: Research guide*. Toronto University Centre for Urban and Community Studies. ED 393544.

Websites

Lakeshore classroom planning, www.lakeshorelearning.com

Resources for Visual Supports

Websites

Do 2 Learn, www.do2learn.com

Use visual strategies for meeting the communication challenges in autism, www.usevisualstrategies.com

Practical autism resources, www.practicalautismresources.com

Visual aids for learning, www.visualaidsforlearning.com

P.O. Box 23173
Overland Park, Kansas 66283-0173
www.aapcpublishing.net

CPSIA information can be obtained
at www.ICGtesting.com
Printed in the USA
LVHW012353040619
620112LV00012B/415/P